your
promising
future

career
development
tools for young
adults

Meta Dunn

jıst
Works
America's Career Publisher

Your Promising Future

© 2004 by Meta Dunn

Published by JIST Works, an imprint of JIST Publishing, Inc.
8902 Otis Avenue
Indianapolis, IN 46216-1033

Phone: 1-800-648-JIST   Fax: 1-800-JIST-FAX
E-mail: info@jist.com   Web site: www.jist.com

Note to Instructors

Support materials are available for *Your Promising Future*. An instructor's guide (ISBN 1-59357-012-0) contains helpful guidance, test questions, and many activities and assignments. Videos and assessments on job search topics are also available. Call 1-800-648-JIST for details.

Visit our Web site at www.jist.com for information on JIST, free job search information, book excerpts, and ordering information on our many products. For free information on 14,000 job titles, visit www.CAREEROINK.com.

Quantity discounts are available for JIST books. Please call our sales department at 1-800-648-JIST for a free catalog and more information.

Acquisitions Editor: Randy Haubner
Development Editor: Barb Terry
Cover Designer: Trudy Coler
Interior Designer and Layout: Aleata Howard
Proofreader: David Faust

Reviewers: Sol Flores, La Casa Norte, Chicago, IL; Suzie Huber, Noblesville High School, Noblesville, IN; Florence Jackson, New York Public Schools, New York, NY; Alice Johnson, Broad Ripple High School, Indianapolis, IN; Toni Lawal, Southwest Tennessee Community College, Memphis, TN; Fred McQueen, Greater Cincinnati Urban League, Cincinnati, OH; Rochelle Perry, Project Return, New Orleans, LA; Beverly Robinson, Arlington High School, Indianapolis, IN; Fidal Young, TRIO Program, Chicago, IL.

Printed in the United States of America

09 08 07 06 05 04 03   9 8 7 6 5 4 3 2 1

ISBN 1-59357-011-2

About This Book

Do you have a promising future? Have you heard "you can't" all your life? Do people constantly point out the obstacles that lie ahead of you? Does "promising future" sound like words that apply to people who live someplace else, or have better grades or stronger families than you do?

Let Meta, the author of this book, show you how you can have the future that you thought was only a dream. She knows what it's like to have heard all the reasons why a successful life is impossible, but she found the courage, strength, and direction that made it possible to begin creating the life she wanted. She is a single mom who made it through to her Master's degree despite the fact that people were telling her to get a job, to settle for less than what she really wanted.

Through the activities in this book, Meta shows you that the source of a promising future lies within you, within the dreams that are who you are. And she doesn't leave you there, with just a bunch of dreams. She shows you how, step by step, to build a future for yourself.

Table of Contents

Introduction

· ·

Discovering your dreams, realizing your potential, finding the job you love, getting ahead, changing your world, and having fun—what do these phrases have in common? They are all components of *Your Promising Future*. Maybe you are reading this because it's part of a class, or maybe you just happened to come across this book and thought it looked interesting so you wanted to check it out, or maybe a friend told you that you might like it. Whatever the reason, this book can help you if you have a dream you want to make come true. If you actually take the time to do the activities and read through the material, you will move yourself in the direction of making that happen for your life.

Unlike other books, though, *Your Promising Future* isn't written for those who are on the right path and just looking for a little motivation. I wrote this book especially for those of you who are living in situations that often seem impossible to overcome. Yes, the principles I share will work for everyone, but if you live in a world like I used to, in which you are struggling to make ends meet and there seems to be no end in sight, this book will speak to you and provide you with the motivation and desire to change your world.

Before you begin, I think that it's important for you to know a little about how to use this book. This is not your typical "how to find a job" book. It has games, activities, real life examples, and journaling-type sections, designed so that you would really think about your life and what it is that you want out of it. Don't do these activities just to get them done or because you were told to, but rather do them with the expectation of creating something new for your life. If you sit down and really let your mind go, you can create a whole new world for yourself. Let go of all those things that hold you back from expressing the real you, and start on the path to changing your world.

The Holla' Zones are your turf.

While you're doing the Holla' Zones, sections in which you can let your thoughts flow, don't worry about how your responses come out. Forget about whether

- Your grammar is correct,
- You make sense, or
- Your ideas sound crazy.

Just write what comes to you—what is on your heart.

The Practice Makes Perfect activities call for accuracy.

Some activities in the book, though, such as the resume and application, are different. The Practice Makes Perfect sections are those that can be used in the "real world." Fill those out with precision because you can and should use them when you step out to find a job.

The rest of the book is for exploring who you are.

For most of the other activities, don't stress. What is most important is that you figure out who you are. If you can't do that, it's not very likely that you'll be happy in any job that you do.

So enjoy yourself as you search your heart and discover who you want to be. Don't get caught up in being right or wrong or even looking good. Just follow your heart!

Throughout this workbook, you learn ways to turn your dreams into realities—if you really want to. If not, it's always fun to dream, right?!? Now, let's get started creating a game plan for your life!

Got Game?

Creating a Game Plan for Your Life

In this chapter, you will

- Create a plan to make your dreams come true
- Overcome the fears that can stop you
- Explore careers that interest you

How often have you sat through some class, lecture, or program supposedly designed to help you succeed in life but because of your situation, you left feeling worse than when you came? You may have been thinking, "Yeah, right. They don't know what my life is like. This won't work for me."

Get to the point:

You probably have heard the words "You can't" far too many times. This chapter shows you that you *can* no matter what circumstance you face.

Maybe you come from a single-parent family, or you are a single parent yourself. Maybe you don't even have a family and are struggling, trying to raise yourself. Maybe you feel as though school is not for you, but you still want to make it, to be a success.

Whatever your situation, you may think, no matter what you read or what advice you get, "that stuff works only for *those* people." You know, *those* people, the ones who have the easy life, are of a different color, have money, didn't make the wrong choices, or didn't have to grow up in the difficult circumstances you did. Well, then this workbook is designed for you!

3

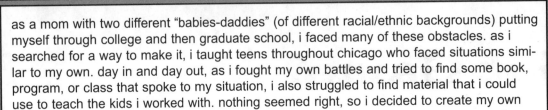

meta - Instant Message

as a mom with two different "babies-daddies" (of different racial/ethnic backgrounds) putting myself through college and then graduate school, i faced many of these obstacles. as i searched for a way to make it, i taught teens throughout chicago who faced situations similar to my own. day in and day out, as i fought my own battles and tried to find some book, program, or class that spoke to my situation, i also struggled to find material that i could use to teach the kids i worked with. nothing seemed right, so i decided to create my own program.

i wrote *your promising future* to provide a hands-on tool to show you that, no matter what you face, you can succeed if you follow your heart. i know because i followed my heart to get to where i am today: in my twenties, two children, a master's degree, with a published book, doing what i love to do—and i stayed on a straight path to do it!

so, if you are looking to succeed in life but haven't found anything to help you, keep reading. *your promising future* is a unique workbook that will help you search your heart and find a life that you enjoy, no matter what you may be going through right now.

Life: The Most Important Game You'll Play

Because you will use this book to guide you to your life's game plan, it's time to get familiar with the topics that we cover. Play this game to help you get started.

This activity introduces you to topics we look at in this book. Read the clue, unscramble the letters, and then write each letter of the correct word in blank line. Some of the letters form two words.

Clue	Scrambled Letters	Your Answer
1. Setting these helps you reach your dreams	osalg	_ _ _ _ _
2. The paper that you fill out when trying to get a job	cliniapopta	_ _ _ _ _ _ _ _ _ _ _
3. Paper that provides a brief background of skills you have to offer a company	emuers	_ _ _ _ _ _
4. Consistently being late for work causes employees to be ____	idref	_ _ _ _ _
5. Section in the newspaper that lists jobs	sdalfsiceiasd	_ _ _ _ _ _ _ _ _ _ _ _ _

Clue	Scrambled Letters	Your Answer
6. The conversation between an employer and a potential employee necessary for obtaining employment	viwtenier	_ _ _ _ _ _ _ _
7. Job search technique cited as the most effective way to find a job	gnowtiernk	_ _ _ _ _ _ _ _ _ _
8. Supervised, on-the-job training for a professional field; usually no or low pay	ipsnenhtir	_ _ _ _ _ _ _ _ _
9. Money for schooling after high school that does not have to be repaid	nastrg	_ _ _ _ _
10. Enlisting in this will provide training, job skills, educational assistance, and the opportunity to defend your country	sacredversmie	_ _ _ _ _ _ _ _ _ _ _ _
11. Financial assistance provided by the government that must be repaid	asnol	_ _ _ _
12. School where you can get an associate's degree or use as a stepping stone to get into a university	ucogmntolileemcy	_ _ _ _ _ _ _ _ _ _ _ _ _ _ _
13. The type of schooling one seeks to develop a specific skill set	doraecolths	_ _ _ _ _ _ _ _ _ _
14. At a minimum, you should aim to obtain this to get a better-paying job or enlist	midolap	_ _ _ _ _ _ _
15. Type of training to help you learn how to start your own business	upalenterenrier	_ _ _ _ _ _ _ _ _ _ _ _ _ _
16. The name of the application you fill out to qualify for financial aid	ASFAF	_ _ _ _ _

You may be asking yourself, "Why should I think about my career path? I'm only in high school. Right now a job is a job, and I'll figure out what I want to do later."

Guess what? That "later" you're talking about is when you realize that you're 40 and miserable, and you can't figure out why you are never happy, why you can't make ends meet, and why you are doing what you are doing. Yeah, 40 sounds like a long time away, but time flies and, before you know it, you *will* be 40. Can you imagine spending all the time between now and then working at a job that makes you unhappy?

In the past, people worked one job for their whole lives, and generations within families often worked in the same occupation. Today many people, especially those in high corporate positions, are rethinking their career choices and changing to something that often pays dramatically less but is more personally fulfilling.

> *The right job makes life better, fits your personality, and reflects who you are.*

They realize that past choices about their careers were for these reasons: "It's what my family does," "My family wants me to do this," "I'll make a lot of money," or "It's the only thing I know about." They now realize that by not considering their career path when they were younger, they are unhappy, overworked, highly stressed, and have little time for relationships with loved ones. So much of their life has been wasted doing something that never produced happiness, despite how much they earned.

Rather than put yourself in that position, if you take time right now to discover what you really want to do you will be able to enjoy the rest of your life. The right job makes life better, fits your personality, and reflects who you are. So why not get on the best path now? This chapter will help you.

Who Says Work Has to Be Boring?

You might be asking, "How can work ever be fun? It's just a means to get the bills paid, right?" Work doesn't have to be boring if you follow your dreams and develop your career plan. Follow these next steps to see how work can become more exciting.

Complete this activity by following each step. The activity will not work if you skip any of the steps, so make sure that you do them in order.

Step 1: Give yourself two minutes to list as many jobs and their duties as you can.

Jobs	Duties

Step 2: Use the following space to come up with a creative way to describe one of the careers you listed. You could draw something, make a collage, write a song, or do any combination of things to present the information.

Step 3: Circle the most appropriate step.

Which step seemed like work?	Step 1	Step 2
Which step was more interesting to you?	Step 1	Step 2

Step 4: Write your answer to the following question.

Why was this step more interesting? _____

_____

_____

When most people think about work, they think of jobs like what you had to do in Step 1—boring work that is done systematically. They aren't excited about what they have to do and do it only because it's required. The reality is that Step 2 is also work, but hopefully you found it interesting because you accomplished the task by using the skills and talents that you enjoy using.

In life, if you think about your interests, skills, and talents as you choose your career, you will be much happier and can often use them in your work. And even if you don't get to do everything you want, you will still be happy because you are doing some of the activities you enjoy.

holla' zone: a place for you to let out your thoughts

stop and think. don't listen to the voices of everyone who says, "you can't." don't listen to what others think you should do. listen to yourself. search your heart. what do you want to do?

take a few minutes to write down all the dreams you have for your life. don't try to figure out how or if you'll accomplish them. just write down everything that comes to mind.

_____

_____

_____

_____

_____

_____

Your Dreams Can Become Real

As a little child, you may have had big dreams for your life that, at the time, seemed totally possible. Right now those dreams are just that—dreams, or that's what everyone tries to tell you. But studies have shown that those who followed their dreams were more successful than those who sought a career for the money. Complete the following exercise to start the journey to your future.

Read each question, and, without thinking too much about it, write what comes to your mind.

1. If you just received $10 million dollars, what would you do with the money? (For example: What would you buy? Who would you help? Where would you travel?) _____

_____

_____

2. List some creative (and legal) ways that you could get paid for doing some of the things you wrote in Question 1. _____

_____

_____

3. If someone told you that you could work any job you wanted no matter how much education or experience you had, what would you do? _____

_____

4. Why would you want to work that job?_____

    _____

    _____

5. What would you be willing to give up in order to make your dream a reality?_____

    _____

    _____

Hard Work and Sacrifice Will Get You There

Now that you have done some dreaming, let's get real. Dreams don't just happen. I know. I can just hear you saying, "What?!? I thought you said I could have what I want."

Well, here's my answer: You can, but it's going to take some hard work and sacrifice. C'mon. It's not very likely that someone is going to just hand you a job or a bunch of money. But when you set your sights to reach your goals and give up those things that will hinder your progress, anything is possible. Yes, that's right; you're gonna have to give some things up, but I promise you it's worth it! Think about how life would be if you didn't have to hustle to get by, constantly look over your shoulder, or hope that so-and-so is going to get it together so you can get some support. Wouldn't a little sacrifice be worth the freedom you'd gain?

Take some time to think about your dreams, and then review the following list. Put a check mark next to the items that you are willing to do to make your dream a reality. Again, don't try to figure out how to make it happen. Just think about whether you would do the following things if doing so meant you could reach your dream.

I'm willing to...

- ❏ Finish high school
- ❏ Get my GED
- ❏ Go to trade school
- ❏ Enlist in the armed forces
- ❏ Volunteer
- ❏ Work as an intern
- ❏ Go to college
- ❏ Go to graduate school
- ❏ Work more than one job
- ❏ Read more

- ❏ Move to a different state/country
- ❏ Be alone for a time
- ❏ Stay up late working or studying
- ❏ Take a class to improve certain skills
- ❏ Cut down on amount of time with friends
- ❏ Let go of past failures/hurts
- ❏ Leave friends/relationships that hold me back

- ❏ Give up certain material possessions until I have reached my dream

Other _____

_____

_____

_____

_____

Don't Let Fear Hold You Back

"The only limit to the realization of tomorrow will be our doubts of today."

– Franklin D. Roosevelt

Think about a goal or dream you have for your future. Can you begin your dream job now? Probably not, but that doesn't mean you should give up on your dream. You probably need additional training or education or to take other steps to get that dream job, which often call for a major change in your life.

Often when we think about the steps it takes to get where we want to be, the task looks huge, scary, and maybe even impossible. On the path, some people give up on their dreams for fear of never being able to make it and then settle for something easier.

Understand that fear is a part of life. Sometimes that fear comes from others telling you "you can't" because of your circumstances. Other times that fear is doubt about your abilities. Whatever the fear you face, you can overcome it and pursue your dreams if you recognize it.

> *Whatever the fear you face, you can overcome it and pursue your dreams if you recognize it.*

Change often involves fear because you don't know what lies ahead, but that is normal. If you are not willing to live with the threat of failure, you will never fail, but you will also never grow.

Read the following list and put a check mark in front of the fears that may be stopping you. Add any fears you face that are not listed.

I have a fear of...

- ❑ Not having enough money
- ❑ Not doing well on tests
- ❑ Not fitting in
- ❑ Not having good/any role models
- ❑ Not liking what you chose
- ❑ Not having parent/family support
- ❑ Facing ethnic/racial prejudices

- ❑ Overcoming poor grades/background
- ❑ Trying to reach a goal when you're already a parent
- ❑ Not being able to handle the responsibility
- ❑ Taking too long to reach your goal
- ❑ Failing
- ❑ Being alone

Other _____

Other _____

Other _____

Other _____

holla' zone: a place for you to let out your thoughts

many times we're afraid to give up something because we're afraid our lives'll be boring or we won't fit in anymore. think about it, though. how exciting is your life now? are the conversations and situations you get into repeats of past situations? or are your conversations about the future? are you constantly seeking new projects? or is life filled with the same ol' drama? if you continue on the path you're on, will you be any closer to reaching your dreams?

in this holla' zone, describe your life in 10 years if you decide you don't want to change how you are living today.

_____
_____
_____
_____

are you happy with that? why or why not?

_____
_____

what could life be like if you stepped out into the deep beyond your fears and followed your dreams?

_____
_____
_____
_____
_____

What Does Success Mean to You?

What motivates you–money or having a purpose for your life? In our society, money tends to be the biggest motivator. Look around. Our lives are swamped with symbols of status and money. One example seen every day is music artists in videos ridin' in Escalades, chillin' in big houses, sportin' nice clothes and jewelry, and partyin' all the time. It would seem that life is easy and wonderful for those who have money.

Then you look at where you are. Being young, you probably don't have a lot of money, the place where you live looks nothing like the houses you see on TV, and as for a car, the city bus or your own two feet may be your only means of transportation. Life isn't just one big party, although at times you wish it could be. You want to be successful in life, but the "successful" lives you see on TV seem far from possible for you. How are you ever going to make it? And how are you going to do it without giving into the temptation of the quick, easy-money solutions that others try to offer you? When you're living in a situation where money seems to be in short supply, you may be even more tempted by money, but if you want to reach your dreams and potential, you can't allow yourself to get distracted by those temptations. So, what do you do?

Look at your definition of success. Everyone has a different way to identify a successful person. Your own personal success is determined by how you define it, so how do *you* determine if someone is successful? This definition can give you some insight on reaching your dreams.

Step 1: In the Signs column, list five signs that you think show someone is successful.

Signs	Source
1. _____	_____
_____	
2. _____	_____
_____	
3. _____	_____
_____	
4. _____	_____
_____	
5. _____	_____
_____	

Step 2: Think about where you got these values (parents, friends, neighbors, or TV, for example). Write the answer in the Source column.

Success Isn't for Chickens or the Lazy

We live in a society where success equals prosperity, but to many of us that type of success seems impossible. Many people start off believing that the dream is real, but in their pursuit, they come up against obstacles.

Unfortunately, when people are motivated by money and times get desperate, they turn to opportunities that turn out to be more harmful than good. Taking the quick way to riches often involves illegal dealings that cause them to have to watch their backs. Or they get into positions that make them unhappy and constantly seek out something that can make them happy. The result can be not only bad for themselves, but also for friends and family, community, and society.

After awhile, those who don't give in to negative pressures may stop dreaming and just settle for life as it is. The truth is that success and prosperity are possible for all, but only those who are willing to face the challenges succeed. If you talk to almost any person who has become successful, you are likely to find out that he or she has faced some tough situations. Complete this worksheet to learn more about success.

The Facts

Think of someone in your life who seems successful to you. Answer these questions about that person:

1. Who is the person? _____ How do you know him or her?

_____

2. What type of work does this person do? _____

3. Why do you consider this person successful? _____

_____

_____

The Interview

Using the following questions, interview this person about how he or she was able to get to where he or she is today.

1. How old were you when you started working? _____

2. What was your first job? _____

_____

3. How many different jobs have you held, and what were they? _____

_____

_____

4. How many years of school did you complete (including school after high school)? _____

5. Are there any special licenses, certificates, or training you had to complete for your position?

_____

_____

_____

6. What is your current job title and what are your duties?

_____

_____

(continues)

(continued)

7. Is this what you dreamed of doing? _____

8. If not, what is your dream job? _____

_____

_____

9. What obstacles have you faced in trying to reach your goal? _____

_____

_____

10. What kept you motivated, especially when it got difficult? _____

_____

_____

11. Would you consider yourself successful? _____

Why or why not? _____

_____

_____

12. What are your goals for the next 10 years? _____

_____

_____

13. What advice would you give someone just beginning his or her career search? _____

_____

_____

The Reflections

After interviewing the person, think about the information you got and answer these questions:

1. Think about the responses given in the interview. How does this person's definition of success give you a different perspective on your definition? _____

_____

_____

2. How can this person's experience help you stay on track for success?

_____

_____

Create Your Own Definition of Success

You've already thought about your beliefs and about what a successful person should look like, but let's re-examine that definition. In the *Webster's New World Dictionary* (published by John Wiley and Sons), success is defined as

> **Success** (n) 1. result, outcome (see also succeed). 2. a favorable or satisfactory result or outcome. 3. the gaining of wealth, fame, or rank, etc.

> **Succeed** (vi) 3. to achieve or accomplish something planned or attempted. 4. to have or enjoy success; realize a goal or goals, esp. in becoming wealthy, winning fame or approval, etc.

Those are the dictionary definitions, but what's yours? Think about your original definition of success, think about your interview with a successful person, and then combine what you've learned with the dictionary definition to create a definition of success for your life. Only you can chart your own success.

Answer these questions according to what you believe in and want for yourself:

1. What is your personal definition of success? _____

   _____

   _____

2. If you were at the end of your life and you looked back over it, how would you determine whether it was successful? _____

   a. What sort of activities would you have participated in? _____

      _____

      _____

   b. What sort of career would you have? _____

      _____

      _____

   c. What would your family look like? (For example, would you married or single, have kids, and so on?) _____

      _____

      _____

   d. Where would you have lived? _____

      _____

      _____

(continues)

(continued)

    e. How much schooling would you have? _____

_____

_____

_____

3. What material objects would you like to have to show your success? _____

_____

_____

4. What areas in your life would you like to see improved? _____

_____

_____

_____

5. By the time you are 19, what success markers would you like to have accomplished in school, work, family, and other areas of your life? _____

_____

_____

6. By the time you are 25, what success markers would you like to have accomplished in school, work, family, and other areas of your life? _____

_____

_____

_____

7. By the time you are 40, what success markers would you like to see accomplished in school, work, family, and other areas of your life? _____

_____

_____

8. Do you have any other dreams you would like to fulfill? What are they?

_____

_____

Now you have a plan to use to determine whether you're on track to the type of success you really want.

holla' zone: a place for you to let out your thoughts

does "giving back" have anything to do with success? read the following scenario and decide for yourself.

two kids from families who are struggling to make ends meet studied hard and focused on school. eventually they got scholarships to top colleges where they earned their degrees and became doctors. one opened a practice in a very rich area of town and bought a large house and nice car. the other student went back to the community she came from and opened up a much-needed clinic. most of the patients at the clinic were on public assistance, so the doctor didn't make a lot of money, but she helped save the lives of many who may have died prematurely if not for the clinic.

which doctor do you think is more successful? why?

_____

_____

_____

_____

_____

truly this question has no right or wrong answers. each doctor has her own purpose for her job. but just because one makes less than the other doesn't mean that she is less successful than the other. her "wealth" comes from the satisfaction of knowing she made a difference in the life of someone who may not have been given an opportunity for life.

finding purpose in your life may take a bit longer than just doing what is familiar to you, but you'll be at peace with your life and know that your efforts not only helped you succeed but also encouraged others to succeed.

Mission Accomplished: Find Purpose in Your Work

Think about the two doctors from the holla' zone again. Remember how I said there was no wrong or right answer, that each one could be considered successful depending on her mission in life? Provided that both enjoyed their work and were not engaging in any illegal activity to get where they were, both should be considered successful because they were fulfilling their own purposes. Often, when people find what it is they are meant to do, they are happy in all areas of their lives. The pieces of their lives that once seemed scrambled all begin to fall into place. This will happen for you when you begin your mission, should you choose to begin to accept it.

According to *Webster's New World Dictionary*, a mission is "a continuing task or responsibility that one is destined, fitted to do, or specially called upon to undertake."

Parts of a mission include

- Making a positive difference in the world.
- Using your talents and abilities in a way that makes you happy and helps to improve the lives of others.

Your mission contains

- The type of work your heart is drawn to.
- The kind of work that most needs to be done in the world.

When you take on the career search process as your mission, your work becomes bigger than you; that is, work no longer is about just bringing home a paycheck and having things for yourself. Rather, work becomes a means to creating change in the lives of others around you. Yes, you still get a paycheck, but the satisfaction that comes from your work no longer occurs just on payday. The joy comes every day from knowing that you've impacted someone's life in a positive manner.

Remember: Your objective is to enjoy what you are doing while making a positive contribution to others. If the work you do violates or abuses other people's freedoms and rights, you are not truly fulfilling your mission. Read these tips to start on your way to accomplishing your mission.

Tips to Keep You on Track

- Write things down. Start a notebook that you can use to record your career change process.
- Be patient. There is no shortcut to finding your mission.
- Be thorough.
- Spend time alone. Set aside at least 15 minutes a day to meditate and to think and write about your career/life investigation process.
- Identify your dreams and values—what is most important in life to you.
- Get involved. Find an organization where you can volunteer. That experience can help identify your likes and dislikes.
- Identify your fears.
- Involve your family.
- Have faith.
- Trust your instincts.
- You may not know exactly what or how to do achieve your goals, but follow your heart and explore your options. Often times when you find what it is you are meant to do, you stumble onto it without even trying.
- Be open to change and new ideas.
- Never give up. You may have times when it looks as if you'll never reach your dreams, but if you stay focused on what you want and keep working, your dreams can come true.

Volunteering: A Way to Discover Life

One way to find out what it is that you really want to do with your life is get involved in activities. You may try some activities and realize that you do not like them. That's fine. We all are not meant to do the same thing. It doesn't matter whether you know someone who likes doing an activity: if it's not for you, don't do it. Find something that you enjoy and keep doing it. It doesn't matter how many different programs you have to try; eventually you will find something you enjoy.

Volunteering provides some great benefits, such as spending time and energy for a cause you believe in, improving your community, helping others, gaining work experience, learning about social issues, being with others who share your interests, and giving you a chance to explore career directions. Although you don't make money from volunteering, the personal satisfaction of knowing you helped support a purpose greater than yourself is another benefit that most will tell you outweighs any financial reward.

Discover the Difference You Can Make

Oftentimes people wonder where they can volunteer. The answer is simple: almost anywhere. Most organizations are excited to have people help them without having to pay them, so the trick is deciding where you want to volunteer and what type of commitment you want to make. To figure out where you should volunteer, complete the following activity.

Circle the answer that best describes your life.

| How often can you volunteer your time? | Once a week | Twice a month | Once a month | During school breaks |

Check the answer that best describes your life.

Are you interested in a yearlong program that pays a living stipend while requiring you to volunteer at a specific community agency?
Yes ❑   No ❑

If yes, check out these sites:
www.habitat.org - Habitat for Humanity
www.cityyear.org - City Year
www.americorps.org - AmeriCorps
www.publicallies.org - Public Allies

Would you like to travel outside the country to volunteer?
Yes ❑   No ❑

If yes, check out these sites:
www.crossculturalsolutions.org - Cross Cultural Solutions
www.peacecorps.gov - Peace Corps
www.globalexchange.org - Global Exchange
www.mar.bg/engpages/index.htm - MAR Bulgarian Youth Workcamps
www.volunteerinternational.org - International Volunteer Programs Association
www.amizade.org - Amizade

(continues)

(continued)

What type of volunteer experience interests you most? (Check all that interest you)	Working with	Working in	Working on
	❑ Animals	❑ Park	❑ Political campaigns
	❑ Elderly	❑ Museum	❑ Justice issues
	❑ Children	❑ Zoo	❑ Crime prevention
	❑ Teens	❑ Theater	❑ Problems in society
	❑ Women	❑ Church	Other_____
	❑ Men	❑ Hospital	_____
	❑ Plants	❑ Nursing home	_____
	❑ Technology	❑ Library	_____
	❑ Autos	❑ Wildlife refuge	_____
	❑ Tools	❑ Botanical garden	_____
	❑ Immigrants	Other_____	_____
	❑ Refugees	_____	_____
	❑ Orphans	_____	_____
	❑ Homeless people	_____	_____
	Other_____	_____	_____

Find Your Volunteering Destination

After you have decided what type of volunteering interests you, explore where you might serve. You don't actually have to volunteer, but you do need to go through the process of looking. Visit one of the Web sites listed in the previous activity, look in a phone book, or put on your shoes and walk around your community.

Find the answers to the following questions.

1. What is the name of the organization that most interests you? _____

   _____

2. What is the mission of the organization? _____

   _____

3. What types of volunteer opportunities does the organization have available? _____

   _____

   _____

4. What sort of commitment do you have to make? _____

   _____

5. What would be your responsibilities? _____

6. What are the benefits of volunteering with this organization? _____

_____

_____

holla' zone: *a place for you to let out your thoughts*

volunteering for an organization or program is a cool way to discover what interests you, gain work skills, and help communities at the same time. sometimes, though, you can't find a place that provides the sort of experience you want. oftentimes a community has needs that aren't even addressed, but with your talents and abilities, you could bring these possibilities to life. think about the many different ways you could help out. use these questions to guide you:

what is the one talent or skill that you enjoy doing the most?

_____

what is the first job that comes to mind in which you could use this talent/skill?

_____

how you could use this talent or skill to help a homeless person?

_____

_____

what are some ways you could use this talent to help a large corporation looking to expand its operations?

_____

_____

how could you use this talent to raise awareness of a community problem, such as the environment, poverty, domestic violence, teen pregnancy, or racial profiling?

_____

_____

(continues)

(continued)

how could you use this talent to help a first grader with his or her studies?

_____

_____

how could you use this talent to help improve your community?

_____

_____

using this talent, what sort of business could you start?

_____

_____

keep thinking of some other ways for using your talent. go beyond what you can see in the world today!

_____

_____

keepin' it real

In the long run, volunteering can pay off. Read this example to see how: Lupe grew up in a large family without a lot of money. She was the first in her family to go to college. As she began school, she still was unsure about what she wanted to do with her schooling, so she began volunteering. While going to school, she worked at various community agencies in the Latino community. Through her volunteering, she discovered the lack of education on financial investing and saving money within the community. Through conversations with the community members she met in her different positions, she began to understand their needs and sought ways to assist them. After graduating from college, a position opened up at a large bank within the community. The position required several years of work experience in the field, which she did not have, but she applied for it anyway. Although fresh out of college, Lupe was given the position because of her understanding of the community members. Her position paid much more than most of her fellow graduating friends received and provided excellent advancement opportunities.

Be Whatcha Wanna Be

While you have already begun exploring your career interests, figuring out what you want to do with your life is like planning a trip. Some people know exactly where they want to go and just have to figure out what is the best, easiest, or cheapest way to get there. Other people know they want to go somewhere but are not exactly sure where, so they have to do some exploring to see which place would suit them best.

No matter where you are on the path to figuring out what you want to do with your life, you are in the perfect place. In fact, sometimes those who have no idea what they want to do end up in very rewarding and successful careers that make them happy. And sometimes those who knew exactly what they wanted to do find themselves very unhappy in their careers and head back to the exploration process.

Don't worry if you don't know what you want to do in the future. If you think you know, always be open to possibilities and learning more—you may end up in a different place than where you started. Looking at all sorts of jobs can help you in your search for the best career for you. In your search, you'll want to find out about the job responsibilities and the salary.

Before you begin researching careers that work for you, see how much you know about some careers that are out there. Following is a list of job titles and a list of their duties and salaries. You will notice some salary ranges are very wide, and you may wonder why. In certain jobs, the type of customer served affects how much you can make. Try to match each job title with its description and salary. Write the number that is next to the job title on the line for the appropriate description.

Job Titles	Descriptions and Salaries
_____ 1. Veterinary technician	a. Serve as stand-in relative, pay bills, make appointments, and visit clients as needed. Salary: $25,000-$85,000+
_____ 2. Event planner	b. Prepare materials, write online help, put technical information into everyday language. Salary: $25,000-$70,000+
_____ 3. Geriatric care manager	c. Design diets, promote healthful eating habits, research nutritional needs. Salary: $25,000-$70,000+
_____ 4. Copywriter	d. Use dance to treat physical, mental, or emotional habits. Salary: $22,000-$55,000+
_____ 5. Radio/TV advertising salesperson	e. Treat physical, mental, or emotional disabilities with the help of music. Salary: $19,000-$48,000
_____ 6. Dance therapist	f. Assist in caring for animals, collect specimens, and assist in surgery. Salary: $18,000-$35,000
_____ 7. Publicity consultant	g. Coordinate colors, styles, and fabrics for customers; offer opinions about merchandise. Salary: $24,000-$68,000+
_____ 8. Music therapist	h. Perform background checks, conduct surveillance, search for missing people. Salary: $20,000-$85,000+
_____ 9. Environmental engineer	i. Prepare food for parties, home meals, and events; serve food; develop themes. Salary: $20,000-$90,000+
_____ 10. Personal shopper	j. Train individuals to use computers, develop curriculum, and answer questions. Salary: $23,000-$55,000

(continues)

(continued)

Job Titles	Descriptions and Salaries
____11. Private investigator	k. Supervise cleanup of contamination and design environmentally safe systems. Salary: $35,000-$100,000
____12. Caterer	l. Design advertisements, including graphics, layout, and artwork. Salary: $18,000-$100,000
____13. Computer and software trainer	m. Write effective, creative copies for print ads, TV and radio commercials, and brochures. Salary: $23,000-$100,000
____14. Personal trainer	n. Sell space to advertisers for commercials. Salary: $20,000-$125,000
____15. Technical documentation specialist	o. Obtain publicity, write press releases, and talk with media. Salary: $20,000-150,000+
____16. Advertising art director	p. Plan and supervise fitness regimes for clients on a one-on-one basis. Pay: $35-$750 per session
____17. Dietician	q. Develop themes for events, choose sites, and negotiate contracts, book entertainment. Salary: $20,000-$150,000+

Let Your Interests Be Your Career Guide

Thousands of types of jobs are available, yet so many people just "do" anything to earn a living. They take whatever comes their way to help get the bills paid, but that's not the best way to live life. When you are working at whatever job opens up for you, there is often little connection between your job and what you enjoy doing, so you spend most of your day doing something that doesn't interest you. On the other hand, knowing what you like and don't like can set you on the path to find the career that's a perfect match for you. Thinking and writing about your interests can reveal a lot about the type of work that would best suit you. You spend most of your life working, so why not enjoy it!

Below is a list of activities and careers that are linked to those interests. Checkmark the activities you enjoy doing and highlight some jobs that sound interesting to you.

Interests	Careers
❑ Perform in drama productions ❑ Create freehand drawings ❑ Attend plays or musicals ❑ Study literature ❑ Write novels or poems ❑ Participate in sports ❑ Write magazine or newspaper articles ❑ Take photographs ❑ Sing ❑ Produce or arrange music ❑ Create dance routines ❑ Teach individuals exercise routines ❑ Play a musical instrument ❑ Write reviews ❑ Create sets/props ❑ Negotiate contracts	**Arts, Entertainment & Media** Photography, Commercial artist, Model, Drama teacher, Architect, Choreographer, Musician, Director, Graphic Designer, Cartoonist, Dancer, Fashion Artist, Art teacher, Singer, Composer, Music teacher, Interior Designer, Actor/Actress, Illustrator, Clothing desiger, Announcer, Sound technician, Set designer, Orchestrator, Make-up artist, Art appraiser, Photo-journalist, Comedian, Communications techni-cian, Copywriter, Editor, Technical writer, Playwright, Columnist, Novelist, Reporter, English teacher, Critic, Interpreter, Translator, Literature instructor, Screen writer, Editorial assistant, Biographer, Lyricist, Humorist, Continuity writer, Freelance writer, Head coach, Professional athlete, Umpire, Sports Instructor, Sports scout, Health club worker, Personal trainer, Jockey, Automobile racer, Motorcycle racer, Sulky Driver
❑ Read science magazines ❑ Study botany (plants) ❑ Study planets and stars ❑ Visit science museums ❑ Study chemistry ❑ Read chemistry articles and books ❑ Collect and study rocks and minerals ❑ Conduct scientific experiments ❑ Study the weather ❑ Research tropical storms ❑ Study ways to reduce water pollution ❑ Study animals ❑ Take soil samples ❑ Study marine (ocean) life ❑ Learn about earthquakes ❑ Create maps ❑ Dig for ancient life/fossils ❑ Study ancient life	**Physical & Life Sciences** Astronomer, Geologist, Meteorologist, Chemist, Physicist, Seismologist, Geographer, Environmental analyst, Metallurgist, Mineralogist, Paleontologist, Geophysicist, Archaeologist, Aerial photographer interpreter, Materials scientist, Environmental research project manager, Geneticist, Sociologist, Historian, Psychologist, Urban planner, Animal scientist, Microbiologist, Physiologist, Food scien-tist, Anthropologist

(continues)

(continued)

Interests	Careers
❑ Treat sick animals ❑ Grow flowers or trees ❑ Keep pets for others ❑ Care for lawns and shrubs ❑ Bathe and groom pets ❑ Study plants ❑ Visit botanical gardens ❑ Breed and raise animals ❑ Fish ❑ Study wildlife	**Plants & Animals** Game warden, Zoo director, Pet groomer, Animal trainer, Dog catcher, Veterinary assistant, Fish farmer, Fish hatchery manager, Organic farmer, Livestock rancher, Bee farmer, Dairy farm manager, Animal caretaker, Stable attendant, Veterinarian, Wildlife biologist, Zoologist, Horseshoer, Horse trainer, Landscape gardener, Horticulturalist, Park naturalist, Forester, Agriculture scientist, Botanist, Tree surgeon, Forest ecologist, Park ranger, Range manager, Lawn service worker, Logger, Yard worker, Soil conservationist, Grounds-keeper, Forest nursery supervisor, Farm machine operator, Farm worker, Cemetery worker, Plant propagator, Tree cutter, Flower nursery owner, Florist
❑ Use logic or scientific thinking ❑ Use numbers to express ideas ❑ Understand and express technical information ❑ Use high-level mathematics ❑ Solve problems using facts ❑ Use computers and the Web to collect information ❑ Write computer programs ❑ Read technical books and articles ❑ Create virtual reality programs ❑ Generate maps ❑ Use the computer to create 3D models ❑ Develop databases	**Math, Engineering, Technology** Computer information systems manager, Database administrator, Computer support specialist, Computer programmer, Web designer, Data communications analyst, Mathematician, Statistician, Actuary, Engineer, Architect, Urban planner, Surveyor, Mapping technician, Building inspector, Industrial engineer technician, Cost estimator, Cartographer, Photogrammetrist, Architectural drafter, Electronic drafter, Laser technician, Broadcast technician
❑ Watch law enforcement programs ❑ Learn about fire prevention ❑ Guard property ❑ Plan public safety programs ❑ Fight fires ❑ Visit a fire station ❑ Study law ❑ Enforce laws ❑ Oversee activities going on in your school/community ❑ Investigate crimes ❑ Fight for the rights of others ❑ Debate	**Law, Law Enforcement, & Public Safety** Lifeguard, Fire fighter, Armed services personnel, Corrections officer, Sheriff, Police officer, Safety inspector, Fire inspector, Ski patroller, Special agent, FBI agent, Special agent, Customs inspector, Security guard, Food and drug inspector, Detective, Equal-opportunity representative, Fire marshal, Police inspector, Fire warden, Wildlife agent, Immigration guard, Bodyguard, Parking enforcement officer, Border patrol, Alarm investigator, Bailiff, Lawyer, Judge, Law clerk, Paralegal, Magistrate, Legal investigator, District attorney, Criminalist, Crossing guard, Financial examiner, Polygraph examiner, Recreational area guard, Parole officer

Interests	Careers
❏ Develop criminal profiles	
❏ Learn about crime prevention techniques	
❏ Eliminate violence in your community	
❏ Save lives	
❏ Protect others	
❏ Study and follow drawings	**Mechanics, Installers, Repairers, & Construction**
❏ Use hand tools and measuring instruments	Home appliance installer, Welder, Tool and die maker, Tool grinder, Electronics mechanic and tech-
❏ Make electrical repairs	nician, Wood machinist, Millwright, Furniture finish-
❏ Set up and operate woodworking machines	er, Locksmith, Machinery maintenance mechanic, Bicycle repairer, Watchmaker, Tire repairer, Auto
❏ Install, repair, and maintain things	mechanic, Auto body repairer, Aircraft engine spe-
❏ Operate and maintain equipment	cialist, Small engine mechanic, Electrician,
❏ Build things	Electrical power line installer, Electrical utility trou-
❏ Fix automobiles	bleshooter, Gunsmith, Heating and air conditioning
❏ Lay brick or tile	mechanic, Construction carpenter, Brick mason,
❏ Repair appliances	Drywall installer, Lather, Pipe layer, Construction
❏ Install flooring	driller, Construction worker, Foreman, Plumber,
❏ Work with your hands	Painter
❏ Paint	
❏ Refinish furniture	
❏ Operate motorboats	**Transportation**
❏ Drive a truck	Transportation manager, Railroad conductor,
❏ Pick up and deliver materials	Airplane dispatcher, Air traffic controller, Traffic
❏ Drive a bus	technician, Pilot, Flight instructor, Motorboat opera-
❏ Fly a plane	tor, Truck driver, Locomotive engineer, Bus driver,
❏ Drive long distances	Parking lot attendant, Taxi driver, Tourist guide,
❏ Operate trains	Airport utility worker, Freight inspector, Ambulance
❏ Drive an ambulance	driver, Subway operator, Train crew member,
❏ Transport people	Stevedore, Chauffeur, Limousine
❏ Set up machines	**Industrial Production**
❏ Use gauges and measuring tools	Printing press operator, Industrial production man-
❏ Do manual labor	ager, Jeweler, Bookbinder, Machine tool cutting
❏ Lift heavy objects	operator, Sewing machine operator, Glass machine
❏ Pay attention to safety rules	cutter, Furnace operator, Chemical equipment ten-
❏ Do precision assembly work	der, Gauger, Production laborer, Welder, Job print-
❏ Inspect, sort, weigh and count products	er, Textile mender, Machine assembler, Grinder,
❏ Operate machinery	Power reactor operator, Pump operator, Crane
❏ Make products	operator, Industrial truck operator, Fork lift driver,
	Portable machine cutter, Electric motor assembler,
	Mold maker

(continues)

(continued)

Interests	Careers
❑ Type ❑ Proofread ❑ Operate computers and other office machines ❑ Study office practices ❑ File letters and forms ❑ Organize and file forms ❑ Type personal letters and emails ❑ Take notes ❑ Learn to type ❑ Write memos ❑ Schedule meetings	**Business Detail** File clerk, Librarian, Administrative assistant, Word processor, Travel clerk, Mail clerk, Shipping clerk, Cashier, Telephone operator, Receptionist, Medical records clerk, Reservations agent, Copyreader, Legal assistant, Archivist, Curator, Legal secretary, Mail handler, Routing clerk, Data typist, Computer operator, Office helper, Collator, Loan clerk, Tax preparer, Payroll clerk, Administrative services manager, Court clerk, Teller, Statistical data clerk
❑ Buy and sell property ❑ Raise money for a cause ❑ Sell products ❑ Persuade others ❑ Call people to sell products ❑ Talk ❑ Promote ideas or products ❑ Make speeches ❑ Create campaigns ❑ Negotiate contracts	**Sales & Marketing** Auctioneer, Advertising agent, Fundraiser, Insurance agent, Wholesale sales representative, Demonstrator, Pawnbroker, Field representative, Real estate agent, Auto sales worker, Travel agent, Public relations specialist, Sales clerk, Lobbyist, Leasing agent, Vendor, Arbitrator, Account executive, Supervisor of sales, Fashion coordinator, Membership director, Sales manager, Telemarketer, Merchandise appraiser, Sales consultant, Marketing manager
❑ Serve food ❑ Cook ❑ Organize parties/events ❑ Help others with their personal appearance ❑ Cut/color/braid hair ❑ Clean ❑ Organize ❑ Plan a trip	**Recreation, Travel, & Other Personal Services** Cook, Baker, Barber, Cosmetologist, Caterer, Flight attendant, Waiter/waitress, Maid, Clerk, Bellhop, Bartender, Counter attendant, Parking-lot attendant, Delivery route driver, Courier, Host/Hostess, Escort, Butler, Nanny, Driving instructor, Desk clerk, Sales attendant, Manicurist, Food service worker, Porter, Gate agent, Caddie, Usher, Bagger, Ticket taker, Lodging manager, Recreation worker, Travel guide, Tailor, Personal assistant, Home care aid, Funeral attendant, Massage therapist, Events coordinator
❑ Counsel people ❑ Lead groups ❑ Work with people in need ❑ Organize activities ❑ Volunteer ❑ Help others ❑ Teach people	**Education & Social Service** Caseworker, Counselor, Teacher, Social worker, Teacher's aid, Anthropologist, Child care worker, Principal, University professor, Marriage counselor, Substance abuse counselor, Job analyst, Rehabilitation counselor, Clergy, Dean of students, Residence counselor, Case aide, Program aide,

Interests	Careers
❏ Study people, cultures, and customs ❏ Assist people in improving their lives ❏ Work with children ❏ Listen well	Educational therapist, Employee assistant specialist, Religious activities director, Training and development manager, Special education teacher, GED teacher, Job counselor, Grant writer, Fundraiser
❏ Develop programs ❏ Be in leadership positions ❏ Serve as an officer of a group ❏ Help others with research ❏ Direct others ❏ Supervise others ❏ Organize activities ❏ Take on multiple tasks	**General Management & Support** Business manager, Personnel manager, Office manager, Funeral director, Food service director, School administrator, Hospital administrator, Retail store manager, Program director, Airport manager, Maintenance supervisor, Executive director, Chief executive of operations, Academic dean, Social welfare administrator, Supervisor, Personnel recruiter, Labor relations specialist, Human resources director
❏ Fill out tax forms ❏ Prepare a budget ❏ Keep records of spending ❏ Set up a filing system ❏ Predict financial trends ❏ Analyze financial records ❏ Watch the stock market ❏ Look up numerical date ❏ Work with numbers ❏ Buy and sell stocks and bonds	**Financial Detail** Accountant, Appraiser, Buyer, Audit clerk, Bookkeeper, Statistician, Financial analyst, Purchasing agent, Billing clerk, Systems analyst, Loan officer, Credit analyst, Controller, Payroll clerk, Securities trader, Auditor, Programmer, Insurance adjuster, Accounting clerk, Brokerage clerk, Claims examiner, Tax clerk, Cashier, Ticket agent, Postal clerk, Toll collector, Controller, Underwiter, Market research analyst, Grants coordinator
❏ Examine specimens under a microscope ❏ Research cures for new diseases ❏ Study health ❏ Help people become healthy ❏ Care for people who are sick ❏ Study the diseases ❏ Volunteer in a hospital ❏ Take biology courses ❏ Diagnose diseases ❏ Do research on plants and animals ❏ Work with children who have a medical condition	**Medical & Health Services** Biologist, Dentist, Microbiologist, Pharmacist, Physician, Optometrist, Chiropractor, Dental hygienist, Speech pathologist, Naturopath, Nutritionist, Physical therapist, Nurse aide, Medical laboratory assistant, Biomedical engineer, Anesthesiologist, Radiologist, Geneticist, Biochemist, Physiologist, Neurologist, Audiologist, Laboratory tester, Orderly, Respiratory therapist, Physician assistant, Midwife, Doula, Nurse, Coroner, Psychiatrist, Athletic trainer, Sports physiologist, Yoga instructor, Massage therapist, Pediatrician, Acupuncturist

This worksheet has been adapted from the Career Exploration Inventory *by John J. Liptak, Ed.D., and the* O*NET Career Interests Inventory *(JIST Works).*

(continues)

(continued)

List five jobs that interest you and tell why you like them.

Job	Why I Like It
1. _____	_____
_____	_____
	_____
2. _____	_____
_____	_____
	_____
3. _____	_____
_____	_____
	_____
4. _____	_____
_____	_____
	_____
5. _____	_____
_____	_____
	_____

You're Sure to Find a Career That Fits You

As you reviewed the lists, you probably came across a few jobs you never heard of or know very little about. Were any of these in the category that seemed to best fit you? Did you write any of these jobs in your top five list? Probably not. People have a tendency to be interested in the things they know something about. Few take the time to find out more about something unfamiliar to them. However, sometimes those unknowns end up being a perfect fit, something we really enjoy. So stop for a minute and take some time to discover a new career. It may be just what you're looking for. If not, it doesn't hurt to know about the career. The next time you run into someone who works in that job, you'll actually have something to talk about!

Look over the job list again. Review the jobs in the category that you find most interesting. Are there any jobs you have never heard about or know very little about?

Step 1: List those jobs on this worksheet.

1. _____
2. _____
3. _____
4. _____
5. _____

Step 2: Choose at least two of those five jobs and find out more information about them. You can look in the Occupational Outlook Handbook by the U.S. Department of Labor, which is available at the library or online at http://stats.bls.gov/oco/ to help with your research.

Job 1 Title _____

Responsibilities_____

_____

_____

Education needed_____

_____

Salary range _____

_____

Job 2 Title _____

Responsibilities_____

_____

_____

Education needed_____

_____

Salary range _____

_____

Be True to Your Values When Deciding on a Career

Now that you have thought of some jobs that might interest you, you should look at other issues that are important to keep in mind when thinking about your future. You need to find a career that not only matches your interests but also your values, favorite activities, and other related points. Later you will also consider your skills and your passions to find a meaningful career for you.

Review the following job-related points to determine which are most important to you and keep them in mind when you are searching for the perfect career. Put a check mark next to the ones that appeal to you.

Workplace Values

- ❏ Working for a cause I believe in
- ❏ Belonging to an organization or group
- ❏ Being creative
- ❏ Having day-to-day contact with the public
- ❏ Setting my own schedule
- ❏ Helping other people
- ❏ Using physical strength and stamina
- ❏ Receiving recognition for my work
- ❏ Having many vacation days

- ❏ Taking risks
- ❏ Traveling
- ❏ Being part of a team
- ❏ Working primarily by myself
- ❏ Working primarily for myself
- ❏ Making my interests my job
- ❏ Working with competition
- ❏ Having good pay, benefits, and job security
- ❏ Working under tight deadlines

Workplace Tasks

- ❏ Working on computers
- ❏ Counseling people
- ❏ One-on-one consultation
- ❏ Presenting to large groups
- ❏ Supervising others
- ❏ Working at a desk
- ❏ Doing the same task for extended periods of time

- ❏ Constantly doing different tasks
- ❏ Doing several tasks at one time
- ❏ Using the phone
- ❏ Working directly with people/customers
- ❏ Helping children
- ❏ Helping the elderly
- ❏ Selling products/services
- ❏ Leading groups

Your Needs

- ❏ Need structure
- ❏ Require exact instructions

- ❏ Think out loud
- ❏ Need to work alone

Your Characteristics

- ❏ Organized
- ❏ An independent thinker

- ❏ A team player

Seek and You Will Find Ways to Turn Your Dreams into a Career

Often people give up on pursuing their interests and dreams because they don't believe they can make money with them. If reaching your dreams is really important to you and you work hard and are creative, you can achieve them. How can you find new ways to convert what started out as just talent into a paying job?

Choose one of your interests; the thing you enjoy doing most—whether it be sports, music, a certain subject, or whatever—and go to either a bookstore or library. Search for books that discuss that particular activity and related jobs.

Bookstores such as Barnes & Noble or Borders have areas for reading and coffee shops inside for customers to sit down and read books without having to buy anything. The stores provide a relaxing environment with a variety of current literature. Oftentimes the information is more current in the bookstores than in libraries, which is why many students use them.

Start your search in the careers section first, and see whether you can find any books that talk about work in the specific are. If you don't find anything there, look for books on that particular topic. If you have trouble finding some books, ask a salesperson or librarian to help. They are usually very knowledgeable and can help focus your search.

When you find a book that discusses different career opportunities in your field of interest, read it to find the different aspects of that field. If you can't find a career book that talks about your interests, think of ways you could start a business of your own in that field.

If you are interested in music, for example, you may find a few books in the careers section, but you will most likely have to go to the section that has books about music. It will probably have a section on how to get into the music industry.

Along with music, many students are interested in jobs related to sports and media. These industries have many different ways for you to get into them; you may not become famous, but you may get to work in an field you enjoy, meet the stars, and make good money doing it.

If you have Internet access, you might want to search online by going to a search engine such as www.yahoo.com, www.google.com, or www.msn.com. Then, in the Search box, type a keyword, such as careers. Research job opportunities in the field of your choice or talk with someone who works in the field you picked. Then complete the worksheet.

Write your answer to these questions about the career that you have studied.

1. What are some jobs in this field that you had not thought about in the past?_____

_____

_____

_____

(continues)

(continued)

2. What does it take to get into this type of career?

   a. How much and what type of schooling? _____

      _____

      _____

   b. What type of work experiences? _____

      _____

      _____

      _____

   c. Does it require any licenses or certificates? _____

      _____

      _____

      _____

3. Are there internship opportunities for this field? Where can you find them? _____

   _____

   _____

   _____

4. What are some specific jobs that appeal to you most and why? _____

   _____

   _____

   _____

5. Are there any professional organizations or networks that people in these fields belong to? If so, what are they? _____

   _____

   _____

   _____

6. What is recommended as the best way to get into this field? _____

   _____

   _____

   _____

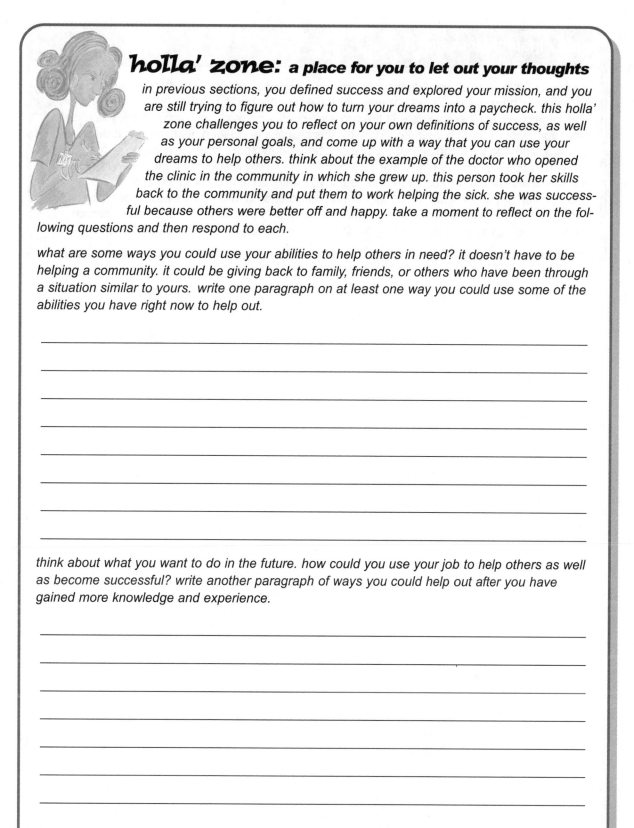

holla' zone: *a place for you to let out your thoughts*

in previous sections, you defined success and explored your mission, and you are still trying to figure out how to turn your dreams into a paycheck. this holla' zone challenges you to reflect on your own definitions of success, as well as your personal goals, and come up with a way that you can use your dreams to help others. think about the example of the doctor who opened the clinic in the community in which she grew up. this person took her skills back to the community and put them to work helping the sick. she was successful because others were better off and happy. take a moment to reflect on the following questions and then respond to each.

what are some ways you could use your abilities to help others in need? it doesn't have to be helping a community. it could be giving back to family, friends, or others who have been through a situation similar to yours. write one paragraph on at least one way you could use some of the abilities you have right now to help out.

_____
_____
_____
_____
_____
_____
_____
_____
_____

think about what you want to do in the future. how could you use your job to help others as well as become successful? write another paragraph of ways you could help out after you have gained more knowledge and experience.

_____
_____
_____
_____
_____
_____
_____
_____

meta - Instant Message

throughout this chapter, you have addressed many issues that come up for people in the career search process. you may or may not have found a career option that seems best for you. regardless of where you are in the process, don't stop now, even if you think you know what you want to do with your life. honestly, this process is life-long. just when you thought you've made it to your goal, a new desire or interest may spark in you, so you'll continue to grow from one vision to another. every step of the way, new fears may try to creep in, different obstacles will need to be overcome, but if you keep coming back to the basics of this chapter, you should be able to conquer them all and end up in a place even bigger than you could have ever imagined. so remember, you've only just begun on the career search mission. don't give up. keep pressing on through each chapter of this book and of your life!

Gonna Stay in the Game?

2

Deciding to Never Stop Learning

In this chapter, you will:

- Find importance in lifelong learning
- Find "life" after high school
- Learn how you can go to college
- Discover various forms of financial assistance

I know what you are thinking, "School is boring. I'm never gonna use most of this stuff anyway. So what does she mean, 'Never Stop Learning'? I don't want to be in school the rest of my life. I don't even want to finish the rest of this year."

> *Get to the point:*
>
> In addition to college, many educational options are available that will help you reach your goals and improve your future.

If I've read your mind, listen up! Learning doesn't have to be boring, and it doesn't have to mean school. Believe it or not, many students who can't wait to get out of high school love their new training or education experiences after they graduate. Whether it's college, job training, or the military, they made the choice, and it is new and interesting. So many options to learn are available that if you can't *get* with the traditional college/university setting, try something different. If you keep reading, you'll find that this chapter provides some creative solutions to bringing your dreams to life, as well as some special tips on how to plan and finance them.

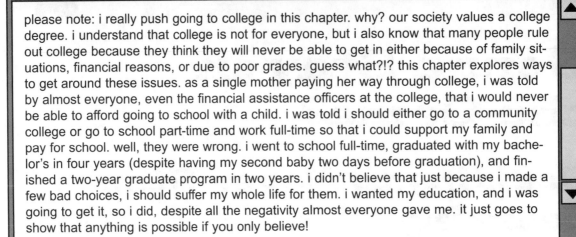

meta - Instant Message

please note: i really push going to college in this chapter. why? our society values a college degree. i understand that college is not for everyone, but i also know that many people rule out college because they think they will never be able to get in either because of family situations, financial reasons, or due to poor grades. guess what?!? this chapter explores ways to get around these issues. as a single mother paying her way through college, i was told by almost everyone, even the financial assistance officers at the college, that i would never be able to afford going to school with a child. i was told i should either go to a community college or go to school part-time and work full-time so that i could support my family and pay for school. well, they were wrong. i went to school full-time, graduated with my bachelor's in four years (despite having my second baby two days before graduation), and finished a two-year graduate program in two years. i didn't believe that just because i made a few bad choices, i should suffer my whole life for them. i wanted my education, and i was going to get it, so i did, despite all the negativity almost everyone gave me. it just goes to show that anything is possible if you only believe!

Why Should I Keep On Learnin'?

Most of us face troubles on a daily basis. Trying to deal with the pressures that come from difficult situations while going to school isn't easy. Often, it seems as though sitting in school is just a waste of time–time that could be spent doing something else that seems to deal more directly with the situations we face. While the value of school isn't always so obvious, the bigger picture of it all is where you can see the benefits. These sections provide insight that will give you a different perspective on making a decision about education.

For this activity, read through the following three scenarios, imagining that they are happening to you, and then think of actions to take that would be beneficial not only for you, but also for society at large. Then answer the questions that follow.

Scenario 1

Despite the Civil Rights Act, (which bans discrimination because of a person's color, race, national origin, religion, or sex), racism still exists in our society. This can be seen by the low levels of minorities in upper-level career positions, poor quality of schools in minority communities, higher rates of imprisonment for people of color, and many other examples. Think of ways you could help in the fight against racism.

1. What are some important steps people could take in order to reduce, eliminate, or prevent racism? _____

_____

_____

2. What are some things you could do right now to help this situation? (Examples: Financially, with your time, organizing people, fundraising, and so on) _____

_____

_____

3. What are some careers you could have that would allow you to help people facing racism?

_____

_____

4. What are some careers you could have that would pay you enough money to be able to help financially? _____

_____

_____

Scenario 2

You are a teen parent. Your baby is three months old, and the baby's mom/dad isn't helping you at all. You are in your junior year in high school, but it's getting difficult to handle all the responsibilities—school, the kid, work—not to mention trying to maintain some sort of a social life. You always dreamed of going to college, but it's getting tough. Think about what you would do.

1. What are some important steps people can take in order to reduce, eliminate, or prevent these problems? _____

_____

_____

2. What are some things you could do right now to help this situation? (Examples: Financially, with your time, organizing people, fundraising, and so on)

_____

_____

3. What are some careers you could have that would allow you to help people facing racism?

_____

_____

4. What are some careers you could have that would pay you enough money to be able to help financially? _____

_____

_____

(continues)

(continued)

Scenario 3

Gangs are an everyday scene in your neighborhood. Normally, you just let it all go. Until now, it's been no big thing—another deal, another war. What can you do? Today, though, it's different. Last night, shots rang out like usual, but this time they hit your best friend, who wasn't even in a gang. Think of what you could do now and in the future to prevent this violence.

1. What are some important steps people could take in order to reduce, eliminate, or prevent these problems? _____

_____

_____

2. What are some things you could do right now to help this situation? (Examples: Financially, with your time, organizing people, fundraising, and so on) _____

_____

_____

3. What are some careers you could have that would allow you to help people facing racism?

_____

_____

4. What are some careers you could have that would pay you enough money to be able to help financially? _____

_____

_____

Know What's Out There

It's going to be hard to make a difference in any of the situations you just read about without some sort of education. These problems are too deep to deal with if you just go off what you know and see right now. So many issues affect each one of these issues that, even with a degree, you're just scratching the surface. While an education isn't going to give you all the answers, it does open your mind to thinking in ways you've never thought before. Education can challenge you and broaden your perspective so that, rather just thinking about the problems you face and finding a solution just for yourself, you can come up with solutions that may have an impact all over the world.

In order to get more education after high school, though, you have to know what's out there. Read over the following types of schools and match them with the correct definition. See how far your mind is willing to expand.

_____ 1. University

a. Offers courses to students from the local area. Often used as a stepping stone to get into a university.

_____ 2. Community College

b. Gives training in shorthand, typing, bookkeeping, and other business subjects.

_____ 3. Graduate School

c. Located outside your home country.

_____ 4. Technical College

d. Focuses on one specific profession.

_____ 5. Trade School

e. Education for cultural and intellectual development rather than as preparation for a specific profession.

_____ 6. Liberal Arts College

f. Several schools within one so that students can receive a wide range of degrees. Usually has graduate programs as well.

_____ 7. Business College

g. Connected to a certain faith denomination.

_____ 8. Career College

h. Has live face-to-face classes taught at two or more locations at the same time, using state-of-the-art, two-way video and audio technology.

_____ 9. Distance Learning School

i. Provides 2-year, 4-year, and/or graduate level degrees in business, engineering, mechanics and/or technology.

_____ 10. Conservatory

j. Allows you to take college courses without ever stepping onto a college campus.

_____ 11. On-line College

k. Teaches skills such as carpentry, electrical work, and plumbing.

_____ 12. International School

l. A division of a university offering classes that will lead you to a Master's and/or Doctorate degree.

_____ 13. Religious College

m. Instruction in music.

Role-Playing: You're the Career Counselor

When you're thinking about your future, you may not give the amount of attention you should to considering the type of school you choose. Often times, we just have too much stuff to do, so we just find out where everyone else is going and apply to the same school. But this could be disastrous for you if your friends and you have different plans for your lives. This activity challenges you to think about how different types of people have different educational needs.

> Here's the scenario: You now have become the school career counselor and want to make sure you are serving your students the best you can. If not, it could mean that you lose your job!

You have talked with four students about their future after high school, but they don't know what type of program would fit them. Read about the different educational options that are available for students and then read the following descriptions about each of the students. Answer the questions in the worksheet, placing each student in the most appropriate setting.

Educational Options

Option	1	2	3	4	5	6
School Name	University Far Away (UFA)	In Town Community College (ITCC)	Local Public University (LPU)	School of Life (SoL)	Overseas Volunteer Program (OVP)	Armed Forces
Location	300 miles away in rural town	15 minutes away	20 minutes away	35 minutes away	Openings in Africa, Asia, and South America	Varies
Type	Private Liberal Arts	Community College	Public research university	Trade school	Hands-on volunteer experience	Hands-on experience in training for military service and over 200 different careers
Population	7,000 under-graduate and 1,000 graduate students. 75% in-state, 20% out of state, and 5% international.	2,500, all from local area.	15,000 under-graduates and 4,000 graduates. 80% in-state, 13% out of state, 7% international.	1,200 students. 96% from local area.		
Student to Teacher Ratio	35:1 in freshman class	20:1	60:1 freshman class	15:1		

Option	1	2	3	4	5	6
School Name	University Far Away (UFA)	In Town Community College (ITCC)	Local Public University (LPU)	School of Life (SoL)	Overseas Volunteer Program (OVP)	Armed Forces
Cost Per Year	$12,000 per year.	$30 per credit hour.	$3,000 per year.	$1,300 per semester.	Travel to and from the country. You receive a small living stipend and financial bonus upon completion of 1 year of service.	Free training (boot camp) with educational and financial benefits. In times of turmoil, you will be on call for duty, so you do have to be willing to give up your life if required.
Housing	$4,000 per semester. On- and off-campus housing accommodations.	No on-campus housing.	$3,000 per semester. Limited on-campus housing.	None.	With a family in the service area or on your own.	Base or civilian options depending on status.
Admission Standards	Top 50% of the high school class with an ACT of 18 or above or an SAT above 1010.	Open— all you need is a high school diploma or GED.	Top 50% of the high school class with an ACT of 18 or above or an SAT above 1010.	High school diploma or GED. An ACT of at least 13. Interview by the program director.	Must be at least 18 years of age. In good health. Interview with recruiter.	Must be at least 18 years of age. Talk to a recruiter. Take the ASVAB— Armed Services Vocational Aptitude Battery.

(continues)

(continued)

Option	1	2	3	4	5	6
School Name	University Far Away (UFA)	In Town Community College (ITCC)	Local Public University (LPU)	School of Life (SoL)	Overseas Volunteer Program (OVP)	Armed Forces
Special programs	Family housing. Daycare facilities for 3 years and older. Study abroad programs. +100 clubs and organizations. Internship opportunities Alternative admissions. Financial Aid for those who qualify.	15 student organizations. Student-run childcare center for infants to 5 years. Several courses that connect with local industries for apprentice-type learning.	+100 clubs and organizations. Research opportunities with professors. Study abroad program. Internships. Alternative admissions program. Financial Aid available for those who qualify.	Financial aid on need-basis only. Specializes in a variety of fields such as carpentry, electrical engineering, and mechanics. Students go through an intensive six-week classroom training session, and then complete the rest of their studies with one class a week combined with hands-on training with professionals in their field. A 15-month program that allows students to get a degree and a real working knowledge of the field they choose to go into.	Can provide academic credit towards college. Have the option to teach English as a Foreign language in middle or secondary schools, assist community members in starting small businesses, develop youth programs, work on projects to raise environmental awareness, raise community awareness for health education, build houses.	Armed forces consists of five branches: Army, Air Force, Navy, Marine Corps, and Coast Guard. The Reserves allows you to enlist in a branch part-time and still go to school or work.

Answer the questions, placing each student in the most appropriate setting.

Student Profiles

Student 1: Darius

Educational background: Junior with a GPA of 2.0 and an ACT score of 21

Activities: Debate team, Student Council, helps organize pep rallies for all the sporting events, captain of the track team, volunteers on the weekends at the local homeless shelter.

Family situation: Darius lives at home with his mother and father, grandmother, and two younger sisters. Both parents work, but neither makes very much money. They are trying to save money to help their children go to school.

School preferences: Darius' motto in life is "The world is my classroom." He really wants to go away for college but is worried about his grades. He hasn't been the best student, but he understands the importance of college and wants the opportunity so that he can become an attorney to fight against the injustices in his community. He is willing to do whatever it takes to get into a good school so he can "be somebody."

1. What option would you suggest Darius selects? _____

2. Why would you place Darius in that program? _____

   _____

3. Would any other option be a good match for Darius? Which one and why? _____

   _____

4. Are there any options you would not recommend for Darius?_____

   Why? _____

   _____

Student 2: Delia

Educational Background: Junior with a GPA of 3.8 and an ACT score of 22

Activities: Delia is not involved in many activities because she has a little 6-month-old baby that she has to take care of.

Family situation: Delia is the first student in her family to get to high school and will be the first one to attend college. Most of her family works in a local factory and does not even speak English.

School preferences: Delia plans to go to college and wants to become a pediatrician. Right now, her aunt helps Delia with the baby while she is in school, but she doesn't know what she will do with the baby when she starts college. The baby's father doesn't help her, and her family thinks she should just work so that she can support herself. Her family won't help her with the baby once she is out of high school if she chooses to go to college—they don't understand the importance of it. Delia is convinced that she needs to go to college and knows that there has got to be some way she can pull it off. Since her family is unwilling to help her out, she thinks maybe she should attend some school out of state so she doesn't have to hear them nag about her decision to go to school.

(continues)

(continued)

1. What option would you suggest Delia selects? _____

   _____

2. Why would you place Delia in that program? _____

   _____

3. Would any other option be a good match for Delia? Which one and why? _____

   _____

4. Are there any options you would not recommend for Delia? _____

   Why?_____

   _____

   _____

Student 3: Joe

Educational background: Senior with a GPA of 1.3 and no ACT score

Activities: None

Family situation: Joe lives with his mother, who works two jobs and attends school. She tries to push him in school, but since she works so much she has little time to keep on his case. She wants the best but feels as though there is nothing she can do anymore, so she just lets him do what he wants.

School preferences: Joe's "not too fond of this thing they call school, you know?" (At least that is what he told you.) He stopped by your office only because the principal made him—or he'd be expelled. Joe is a "hands-on type of guy" who doesn't like to be talked down to. He thinks that none of the stuff in the classroom really applies to "out there" (you know, the "real world"). If he were going to go to college, it would have to be where he could learn by doing. He thinks maybe he could get into learning if it actually had something to do with life and getting a job. You asked him if he would be willing to come see you one other time, and you promised to have some information on schools that may be able to provide him that sort of experience. He seemed interested and promised he would be back next week, but if you didn't have anything good, that would be the last time he'd be back.

1. What option would you suggest Joe selects? _____

   _____

2. Why would you place Joe in that program? _____

   _____

3. Would any other option be a good match for Joe? Which one and why? _____

   _____

4. Are there any options you would not recommend for Joe? _____

Why? _____

_____

_____

Student 4: Lety

Educational background: Junior with a GPA of 3.2 and an ACT score of 20

Activities: Church youth group, swim team, volunteers at local community development organization

Family situation: Lety lives with her father and younger sister. Her mom died when she was 12. Her father works long hours, occasionally traveling outside of the U.S. for his work. Because of her father's work, Lety is very interested in international affairs and helping communities grow.

School preferences: Lety believes that education isn't determined by the type of school you go to but rather by the experience you gain in whatever you do. She is interested in college but would also consider other options for a more hands-on learning experience. She would love to travel, learn, and help others all at the same time.

1. What option would you suggest Lety selects? _____

_____

2. Why would you place Lety in that program?

_____

_____

3. Would any other option be a good match for Lety? Which one and why? _____

_____

_____

4. Are there any options you would not recommend for Lety? _____

Why? _____

_____

_____

Don't Get Left Behind

Education can be the key to changing your life. Many people are stuck in negative situations because they don't have the income to get them to a better place. Often they need more education before they can increase their income.

Think of people you either know personally or have heard about who face situations similar to ones discussed in the previous activities: situations in which they struggle and know that one of the biggest barriers to overcoming the situation is not enough education or training. These people know that if they had degrees or specific training they could get better jobs and get out of their situations. Because they don't know how to make getting an education possible, they just stay in the situation they are in.

Answer the following questions about someone you know who is staying in a tough situation.

1. What is this person doing now? _____

_____

2. Has his or her life seemed to improve in the last two years? _____

How can you tell?_____

3. Does he or she still want to go back to school? _____

4. How might going back to school benefit this person? _____

_____

5. From what you have learned from this book so far, what advice would you give this person?

_____

_____

holla' zone: a place for you to let out your thoughts

imagine this: it's the end of senior year. you have decided to go to college, and you have been accepted at your first choice school, which is out of state. you are very excited to go, but you just found out that your mom, the sole bread-winner for the family, just lost her job. with the way the economy is right now, who knows when she'll find work. she never finished high school and made the salary she did in her last job only because she had been there so long. she says she really wants you to go to college, but you know that she'll be struggling to pay the bills if she doesn't find a job soon. what do you do? do you still go off to college? do you decide to stay home and go to a community college for a year or two so you can go to school and work to help support your mom? do you completely put off school to stay home to help pay the bills? explain your choice and some of the possible outcomes.

_____

_____

_____

there is no right or wrong choice in a situation like this. the best decision can often be reached only after a long conversation between your family and you. sitting down and discussing the options will help you both make a decision that you can be comfortable with in the long run. no matter what your decision, you have to trust that you all are going to get through the situation and in the end come out on top. it is through the tough times that we all grow stronger.

Say *What?!?* Me Go to College?

When trying to decide whether more schooling is right for you, you need to consider many issues. The following information will provide you with a brief glimpse of some of the important factors to consider when making a decision about higher education.

Do you feel as though you cannot or do not want to go to college because you don't think you qualify or there is not a school that is suitable for you? If these fears are holding you back from going to college, you need to read on because a school is available for every need.

In the end, remember, going to college is not just about earning a degree; it's a decision that impacts your whole life. College opens up the doors not only to new job opportunities but also new life opportunities as well. As you read, keep your mind open to the possibilities that could open up for you.

You Make the Decision

College is not for everyone, but it has benefits. Use the following questions to help you think more about whether college may be an option for you.

Write your answers to the following questions.

1. List some of the people you know who have gone to college and tell why they chose to go to college.

Names	Reasons for Going to College

(continues)

(continued)

2. List other people you know who haven't gone to college and tell why they didn't go to college.

Names	Reasons for Going to College
_____	_____
_____	_____
_____	_____
_____	_____
_____	_____

3. How do you feel about going to college? _____

_____

4. How might going to college help you? _____

_____

_____

5. What will you do if you don't go to college? _____

_____

_____

6. What are some alternatives to college that could provide you with training for a career?

_____

_____

The Possibilities Are Endless

If you like to be around a lot of people and are into performing arts, you will not be happy going to a small business school in the middle of Iowa. Yet if that is the only school you know about and you end up at that school, you will probably be miserable and either drop out or gain very little from your education. The key to a successful and fulfilling education is learning the different options available and choosing the one most appropriate for you. Schools come in all sizes, address all fields of study, and provide a range of opportunities for students. Here are some of the different factors to consider when trying to decide if and what type of school you would like to attend. Read through the following lists and check off those items that interest you. Remember, you can choose as many as you want in each section; it is always best to keep your options opened.

Location

College is the perfect opportunity to expand your borders. This could mean staying close to home and learning more about new things and places, or it could mean a whole lot more. Some people have never traveled outside their own city, so going to college in a different town, state, or country may be an option to help them get out and broaden their horizons. Think of where you would be most comfortable and seek out schools in that area. The following questions will help you place yourself.

Maybe you would like to travel to a different country. The world is yours to choose from.

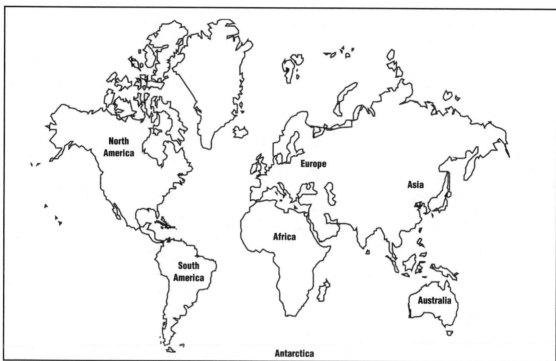

Highlight some areas that may interest you.

1. Which continent might you be interested in traveling to?_____

_____

_____

_____

_____

_____

_____

_____

_____

_____

(continues)

(continued)

Look over the map and list of states to help jog your geography memory. Put a check next to the states that interest you and highlight them on the map.

Answer the following questions.

2. How far away from home do you want to live? _____

    ❑ Less than one hour   ❑ Up to 3 hours

    ❑ 1-2 hours away   ❑ More than 3 hours away

3. If you are looking out of state, which state(s) would you prefer to live in? _____

    Why? _____

    _____

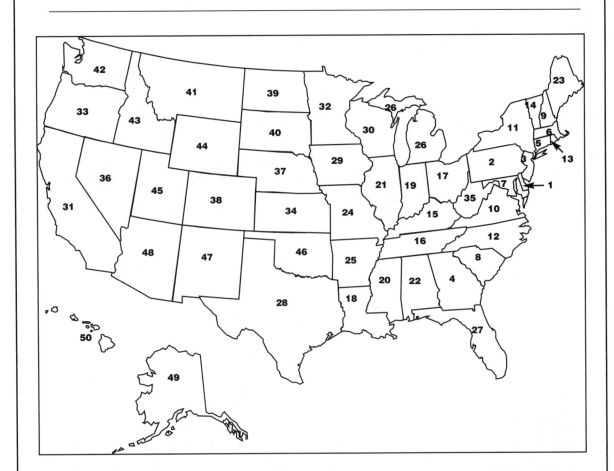

❑ 1. Delaware   ❑ 5. Connecticut   ❑ 9. New Hampshire
❑ 2. Pennsylvania   ❑ 6. Massachusetts   ❑ 10. Virginia
❑ 3. New Jersey   ❑ 7. Maryland   ❑ 11. New York
❑ 4. Georgia   ❑ 8. South Carolina   ❑ 12. North Carolina

❑ 13. Rhode Island	❑ 26. Michigan	❑ 39. North Dakota
❑ 14. Vermont	❑ 27. Florida	❑ 40. South Dakota
❑ 15. Kentucky	❑ 28. Texas	❑ 41. Montana
❑ 16. Tennessee	❑ 29. Iowa	❑ 42. Washington
❑ 17. Ohio	❑ 30. Wisconsin	❑ 43. Idaho
❑ 18. Louisiana	❑ 31. California	❑ 44. Wyoming
❑ 19. Indiana	❑ 32. Minnesota	❑ 45. Utah
❑ 20. Mississippi	❑ 33. Oregon	❑ 46. Oklahoma
❑ 21. Illinois	❑ 34. Kansas	❑ 47. New Mexico
❑ 22. Alabama	❑ 35. West Virginia	❑ 48. Arizona
❑ 23. Maine	❑ 36. Nevada	❑ 49. Alaska
❑ 24. Missouri	❑ 37. Nebraska	❑ 50. Hawaii
❑ 25. Arkansas	❑ 38. Colorado	

Campus Setting

The type of community where your school campus is also plays a part in the total college experience. Each campus setting offers different activities and introduces you to different types of people. You need to consider factors such as these: Do you need to be around people with different backgrounds, values, and so on? Are you looking for a campus where you'll fit in? Or do you mind being "one of the few" on campus? Think about the campus setting. Which would you prefer?

Checkmark the setting that appeals most to you.

❑ *Urban campus*   ❑ *Suburban campus*   ❑ *Rural campus*

Types of Schools

Schools come in all shapes and sizes. Following are different types of schools. Which one would suit you best?

Put a check mark next to of those schools that interest you.

❑ **Large universities.** Large universities offer a wide range of educational, athletic, and social experiences. Universities offer a full scope of undergraduate majors and award Master's and Doctoral degrees as well.

❑ **Private universities.** Some large private universities are well known for their high entrance standards, the excellence of their education, and the success rates of their graduates. These institutions place a great deal of emphasis on research and compete aggressively for grants from the federal government to fund these projects.

❑ **Public universities.** Large public universities also support excellent educational programs, compete for and win research funding, and have successful graduates. Public universities usually offer substantially lower tuition rates to in-state students, although their tuition to out-of-state residents are often comparable to private institutions.

❑ **Liberal arts colleges.** If large universities don't appeal to you, you may find a small liberal arts college a better match. A liberal arts college generally has a smaller student population—generally less than 5,000. The mission of most liberal arts schools is learning for the sake of learning and applying your education to any number of careers. Liberal arts colleges also provide an environment where the faculty and the students get to know each other.

❑ **Small universities.** Smaller universities often combine stringent admissions policies, hand-picked faculty members, and attractive scholarship packages. The number of students who attend these universities remains around 4,000. The choices in courses vary, but not to the extent that they do at a larger university.

❑ **Religious colleges.** Many private colleges have religious origins, and many of these have become secular institutions with virtually no trace of their religious roots. What sets religious colleges apart is the way they combine faith, learning, and student life. Faculty members and administrators are hired with faith as a criterion as much as their academic credentials.

❑ **Specialized colleges.** Another alternative is the technical/specialized college. Their goal is to offer a specialized experience in a specific field or subject. Such a college might limit its course offerings to engineering and science, the performing arts, or business. Some institutions are strong believers in the necessity of focused, specialized study to produce excellence in their graduates' achievements. If you are certain about your chosen path in life and want to concentrate on subjects such as math, music, or business so that you may be best prepared for a specific career, a specialized college may be the choice for you. The next section addresses these options even more.

❑ **Niche schools.** There are also schools that are specific to certain racial and gender groups, such as historically black, single gender, and Hispanic schools. Would any of these interest you?

School Focus

Some people choose a school based on what it's "known for" or the programs it has. If you want to attend college football games, don't consider attending a school that doesn't even have a team! Here are some other areas you may want to consider in the school you choose.

Put a check mark next to those areas that interest you.

❑ Strong academics

❑ Sports orientated

❑ Arts

❑ Research institution

❑ Fraternities and sororities

❑ Clubs and organizations

❑ Volunteer and internship opportunities

Competitiveness or Entrance Difficulty

Colleges vary on level of difficulty for admissions. Not everyone has the desire or grades to make it into a school like Harvard, but everyone has the opportunity to go to college. The following entrance checklist will help you decide which college will fit your academic levels. Remember, entrance difficulty shouldn't always stop you, especially if you fall into a minority group. Some of the tougher schools have special programs to increase their minority enrollments!

Put a check next to the entrance standards you meet.

❑ **Most difficult.** More than 75 percent of current freshman are in the top 10 percent of their high school class and have +1310 on the SAT or +29 on the ACT. About 30 percent or fewer applicants are accepted.

❑ **Very difficult.** More than 50 percent of freshmen are in the top 10 percent of high school class and have +1230 on the SAT or +26 on the ACT. About 60 percent or fewer applicants are accepted.

❑ **Moderately difficult.** Most current freshman are in the top 50 percent of their high school class and have +1010 on the SAT or +18 on the ACT. About 55 percent or fewer applicants are accepted.

❑ **Minimally difficult.** Most current freshman are not in the top half of their class and scored somewhat below 1010 on the SAT or 18 on the ACT. Approximately, 95 percent of applicants are accepted.

❑ **Noncompetitive.** Virtually all applicants are accepted regardless of high school rank or scores. Many public institutions are required to admit all state residents.

Services Provided

Are there certain accommodations that would be necessary to help you in going to school? Some of the following may be important in considering your options as well.

Put a check next to any need you may have.

❑ Campus housing   ❑ Transportation/parking

❑ Day care services   ❑ Services for disability

❑ Family housing

Cost

The cost of education isn't just tuition. Housing, meals, books and other fees also play into the financial web. While cost is an important factor, you should never eliminate a college based solely upon the cost. Remember there's always the potential of financial assistance, discussed later.

Alternative Admissions Programs

Now I've got you thinking. *So what* if you live in the middle of the 'hood, or your parents are making you pay for school. College might actually be a good investment for you, right? But wait. Right now you're saying, "I've never thought about going to college, so I never paid attention to my grades and now there is no hope. I'm almost finished with high school. There's nothing I can do." Wrong! There is always hope! Yes, it might take some extra work on your part, but isn't it worth the extra effort now rather than living for years unhappy and in the same situation you are currently in?

Many colleges have alternative admissions (AA) programs that provide enrollment opportunities for high school or college transfer applicants who do not meet the regular admissions requirements of most colleges or universities (often due to poor grades or test performance). The programs are open to anyone who has the motivation and desire to succeed in college.

To see whether you are candidate for an alternative admission program, read through the following list and decide which one statement in each of the three categories that most applies to you.

Put a check next to one statement in each category.

Category	Low	Average	High
Grades	❑	❑	❑
Test scores	❑	❑	❑
Motivation	❑	❑	❑

Put a check next to this statement if it is <u>true</u> of you.

❑ Did you previously have good grades, but your performance fell due to a personal or family situation?

If you checked High in at least one category and Low in at least one other category or you checked the last statement, an alternative admission program may be just what you need! Talk with your school counselor or perspective colleges for more information. Even if the college you choose does not have an AA program, ask if it offers any alternatives for you. Often being persistent shows that you are motivated enough to complete your studies.

Hundreds of schools throughout the country offer alternative admission programs, but few people know about them. Call any schools you are interested in attending to see if they have any alternative admissions policies. It could be that the school you thought was impossible to get into is actually easier than you imagined.

holla' zone: **a place for you to let out your thoughts**

take a moment to reflect on college. if you could design your own college experience, what would it be like? think of the different factors mentioned in this section and write a description of the ideal college for you.

_____

_____

_____

_____

_____

What If I Can't Hang with College (Just Yet)

You've worked through the college section, you've thought about all the issues in it, and you've decided that college just isn't for you. It's not about grades, money, or programs–you just don't think college is what you want to do, or at least not right now. You may just want time away from school. Or maybe you feel you need more experiences to figure out exactly what it is you want to do with your life. Or maybe you just like to learn by doing, not by studying. If so, then this section is for you!

Everyone Has Options

You have plenty of options in addition to college. Everyone's situation is different. Keep in mind that, while many careers require a college degree, jobs are available for those who do not want to or may not be able to attend college for four years. Because many of these options involve specialized training programs, you need to think about the types of skills you want to develop as well as the school.

Complete this word search to find just a few of the options available to you, using the list on the next page.

```
R E D I V O R P E R A C D L I H C C O G Y H I A
L O N H C E P H E T O G R P H O T O G R A P H Y
E E A T A C I O M U S I K F S D A N C A E E O H
C D I W R N A T D R M M B A S G I S A P C L T F
T A L Y M U S I C G E A D S C B S T S H H E E K
E N T R E P R E N E U R S H I P T R A I N I N G
C C E C D A R T N E P E U I N O I T A C U D E P
H E C L S R M N R T T N S O A T E G S A I C M T
N H H A E A E D U K R A H N H R D N O R L T A R
O O N S R L D E C R O E I D C A C I C T D R S W
L T I S V E I N T H S H N E E N A B I D C I S S
O E C I I G C T I O L I E S M I T M A E A C A E
G L I E C A A E O T O E N I E N I U R S R I G S
Y M A S E L E L N E G M S G C G O L E I E A E S
E E N E L E C T R I C I A N H I N P A G Z Z T A
L N D D E N T A L A S S I S T A N T L N W Y H L
E A H O T E L M A N A G E M E N T V E V V R E C
C G F C H I L D C A Y G O L O T E M S O C A R E
N U R S I N G I F I L M P R O D U C T I O N A N
E M L E E R G E D S E T A I C O S S A I D I P I
C E M M E D I C A L A S S I S T A N T E M L I L
A A R T A N D D E S I G N C O S M E E T O U S N
N C O N S T R U C T N O I T C U R T S N O C T O
```

❑ Armed service

❑ Art and design

❑ Associates degree

❑ Childcare provider

❑ Construction

❑ Cosmetology

❑ Culinary

❑ Dance

❑ Dental assistant

❑ Education

❑ Electrician

❑ Entrepreneurship training

❑ Fashion design

❑ Film Production

❑ Graphic art design

❑ Hotel management

❑ Massage therapist

❑ Mechanic

❑ Medical assistant

❑ Music

❑ Nail technician

❑ Nursing

❑ Online classes

❑ Paralegal

❑ Photography

❑ Plumbing

❑ Real estate

❑ Technology

Find Out What's There

A variety of types of training programs are available—so many that reading the list would get boring. So, rather than just reading about the programs, it's your turn to find out what's out there. Choose one of the fields from the preceding word search and find out more about what it takes to get into that field. If none of those fields seem interesting, check out the following list for a few more. After you have chosen your field to research, answer the questions in the worksheet.

- Carpenter
- Flight attendant
- Home-care aide

- Police patrol officer
- Surgical technician
- Truck driver

Answer the following questions about the career field you have chosen to research.

1. What field are you researching? _____

2. What type of schooling do you need to get into that field? _____

   ❑ One class   ❑ Associates (2-year) degree

   Other _____

3. What certificate or degree will you have upon completion of that course? _____

   _____

4. What will you be able to do with that certificate or degree? _____

   _____

   _____

(continues)

(continued)

5. After you complete of your schooling, do you have to complete ongoing training to continue in that field? _____

   If so, what kind? _____

   _____

6. What is a typical salary range for this field? _____

   _____

---

holla' zone: *a place for you to let out your thoughts*

whatever your decision, it's obvious that some sort of training/schooling is going to be necessary in order for you to succeed in life. so, how much can you take?

how long are you willing to go to school? _____

how far in life can you realistically go with that? _____

_____

_____

is that enough for you? why or why not? _____

_____

_____

Show Me the Money

Whether it's college, trade school, or another training program, this whole school thing is beginning to look more like a possibility, but it still costs so much. People say, "Don't look at the price tag," but how can you not? You don't have any money, and most of these programs cost. You know they're not going to let you in just because you're cute, so what can you do? Sure, you've heard people talk about the FAFSA and scholarships, but what does that have to do with you? The answer: A lot! Read on and find out more about financial aid and how it can help you get a postsecondary education for next to nothing.

The Truth About Money for School

Several myths are out there about the whole financial aid process. Quiz yourself on how much you know, and then read through the answers to find out the whole story.

Circle either True or False.

1. Financial aid is loaned money that you have to pay back.   True   False

2. To qualify for financial aid, you just have to fill out an application.   True   False

3. The FAFSA is an application provided by the federal government to help determine an individual's ability to pay for schooling.   True   False

4. The FAFSA determines the cost of school.   True   False

5. The amount of money you are expected to pay for school is determined by both your family's and your income and assets.   True   False

6. If you are paying for schooling on your own, the FAFSA doesn't require your family's income and asset information.   True   False

7. The total cost of a school is reflected in the tuition.   True   False

8. The amount of money the FAFSA says you will pay for school stays the same, no matter if you go to a school that costs $1,000 or $10,000.   True   False

9. Work Study is one form of financial aid.   True   False

10. The only financial assistance you will receive is what is determined by the FAFSA.   True   False

11. You can get a FAFSA form only from the college you will be attending.   True   False

12. You can fill out the FAFSA only after a college has accepted you.   True   False

13. You have to apply for financial aid only one time as long as you don't stop going to school.   True   False

14. There is no way to reduce how much you are expected to pay for school.   True   False

Now that you've taken the quiz, check your answers to see whether you know the truth about financing schooling. Be sure to read the explanations so that you understand why the myths are wrong.

1. *Financial aid is loaned money that you have to pay back.*

   False: Financial aid is money to help a family bridge the difference between what the family is able to pay and what the school costs (see Number 3 for more details).

   Financial aid comes in various forms, some as loans that have to be repaid, but other is free money. We discuss more about these options later.

2. *To qualify for financial aid, you just have to fill out an application.*

   True: To determine whether you qualify for aid, you just have to fill out the FAFSA form.

3. *The FAFSA is an application provided by the federal government to help determine an individual's ability to pay for college.*

   True: The Free Application for Federal Student Aid (FAFSA) is an application provided by the federal government to help determine an individual's ability to pay for schooling. A specific formula is used to assess how much your family can afford to pay for school. Using the amount derived from the formula, the FAFSA then looks at how much the school costs (TC) and determines what the family is expected to pay for school (Expected Family Contribution or EFC)and what the school is expected to come up with. The difference between these two numbers (TC and EFC) is your financial need.

   The following formula might make this clearer:

   ```
        Total Cost of school
   –    Expected Family Contribution
        (determined by the FAFSA)
   _____
   =    Financial need
   ```

   Here is an example:

   The cost of tuition, room and board, and books for University Far Away is $13,500 per year. The FAFSA determines that your family can afford to pay up to $5,000 for college, so your financial need is as follows:

   ```
        $13,500
   –    $ 5,000
   _____
   =    $ 8,500
   ```

   So, the school would have to come up with $8,500 in loans, grants, scholarships, and/or Work Study so that you could afford to go to that school. The less you can get in loans, the better it is for you.

4. *The FAFSA determines the cost of school.*

   False: The school sets its tuition. The FAFSA determines your Expected Family Contribution (EFC), which tells schools how much of the tuition and fees you will be able to pay.

5. *The amount of money you are expected to pay for school is determined by both your family's and your income and assets.*

    True: Your EFC is determined by the following information:

    - Family's available income

    - Family's available assets

    - Student's available income

    - Student's available assets

6. *If you are paying for schooling on your own, the FAFSA doesn't require your family's income and asset information.*

    False: Unless you are

    - Over 24 years old,

    - Married,

    - Have a child, or

    - A foster child or ward of the state.

    The FAFSA calculates your family's information as well. It is the government's belief that your family will assist you, even if that is not what is true. But, if you fall under any of the above categories, you qualify as an independent and then only your (and your spouse's if you're married) income is used in the calculation.

7. *The total cost of a school is reflected in the tuition.*

    False: The total cost of a school is calculated by the FAFSA using the following numbers:

    - Tuition and fees

    - Room and Board

    - Personal expenses

    - Books and supplies

    - Travel expenses

8. *The amount of money the FAFSA says you will pay for school stays the same whether you go to a school that costs $1,000 or $10,000.*

    True: Regardless of whether the school you apply to costs $10,000 a year or $1,000, if your EFC is calculated to be $3,000, your family is expected to be able to pay up to $3,000 for school. At the first school, you would qualify for $7,000 in financial assistance, but at the second school you would not qualify for any assistance.

9. *Work Study is one form of financial aid.*

    True: Work Study is just one form of financial aid. Students can qualify for aid from more than one source. Some sources provide free money you don't have to pay back or earn. Others consist of work or pay-back loans. Be sure to look into all options and choose the ones that work in your situation.

The three types of financial aid are

- Grants and Scholarships: These don't have to be paid back. They are FREE MONEY.

  Grants are given by the government. The amounts are determined by family need, as shown on the FAFSA (see section on FAFSA for further info).

  Scholarships can be offered through the school or outside sources. You may have to fill out separate applications for scholarships.

- Federal Work Study (FWS): Provides part-time jobs to students (usually on campus, but other jobs qualify as FWS as well). The money earned is put toward either tuition or living expenses. (You really don't see the money, even though you are working.)

- Student loans: Money borrowed from the federal government to help pay for school. Loans are either subsidized or unsubsidized. *Subsidized* means you don't have to pay any interest on the loans until after you finish or leave school. The interest rates of these loans are often much lower than those of most loans. *Unsubsidized* loans start accruing (charging) interest as soon as you take them out, so try to avoid them.

10. *The only financial assistance you will receive is what is determined by the FAFSA.*

   False: You can find other ways to get more money than what is offered as a result of your FAFSA. Following are a few tips:

- It is possible to negotiate financial aid packages. The key is to be friendly, in control, and firm with the financial aid officer (FAO).

- FAOs and FAFSA forms often use terms that are confusing to most people. Unfortunately, many people don't ask questions to clarify these terms and wind up paying more than they need to for school. Don't let the strange terms intimidate you. Just keep asking questions until you understand.

- Almost all colleges hand out their own grants. If a FAO says federal regulations control how much they give, that is not true. Just press on and keep asking for more.

- Apply for scholarships. You can apply for as many scholarships as you would like. If you work hard enough, you could receive more money that what it costs to go to school!

11. *You can get a FAFSA form only from the college you will be attending.*

   False: The FAFSA is available from your high school guidance counselors and from public libraries. Schools do provide FAFSA forms as well, but generally only for students already attending their school.

12. *You can fill out the FAFSA only after a college has accepted you.*

   False: You can fill out the FAFSA after January 1 of your senior year in high school (or the January before you need financial aid). You need to complete the FAFSA after you fill out your tax forms, so figure your taxes early. The sooner you turn in your FAFSA, the more money you are likely to receive as some grant money goes on a first-come, first-serve basis.

13. *You have to apply for financial aid only one time as long as you don't stop going to school.*

   False: You must reapply for aid every year—which could be good or bad if your situation changes.

14. *There is no way to reduce how much you are expected to pay for school.*

False: There are some ways to reduce your Expected Family Contribution (EFC), which will reduce what you are expected to pay. First, figure your taxes and then fill out financial aid forms. The following items on your tax forms help determine your need, so it is important that you pay special attention to them.

- Line 33 on your tax form (adjusted gross income) is a big factor in determining how much money you can afford for school. You want this figure to be as low as possible.

- Some families can get an automatic $0 Expected Family Contribution (EFC)–the government allows this for families who make less than $13,000 per year and are eligible to file the 1040A or the 1040EZ tax form. These families qualify for a complete financial package.

- If this year's income is not representative of the true family income (you've had a good year, but it's not usually so high, and it won't be so high next year), write to your FAO and let the person know. Include a copy of the previous year's tax return.

The following tips provide additional information about the financial aid process. Knowing this information can help you through the financial aid process and possibly put more money back in your own pocket.

Tips About Financial Aid

- Education is a business, and schools need money to stay in business. They try to get as much money from families as possible. An article in *Money* magazine showed that 65% of private institutions and 27% of public universities now engage in financial leveraging (figuring out how little aid they need to award to still get the student to enroll). If you know how to play their game, you'll get more money.

- Financial aid forms calculate family need (called a needs analysis). The family is not allowed to make the calculation nor is it told about how the calculations are formed.

- Never accept the initial offer of a financial aid package. Most colleges aim to give lower than what they can.

- Often the people who get the most aid are those who understand the aid process, not those with the greatest need.

- Sometimes those families who make $35,000 per year, rent a home, and have no assets can get a better financial aid package from an expensive private school than they could from a less expensive state school.

- Do not pay for an award search program—most are scams.

Don't Overlook Scholarships

Next to grants, which you can get only if you qualify, scholarships are the best option for paying for school. Thousands of scholarship opportunities are available, and you don't have to have good grades to qualify for all of them. Following are some sources to tap into when looking for scholarships. Also visit a bookstore or library to find many books filled with scholarship opportunities.

- **Minority status.** This includes not only race or ethnicity, but also gender.
- **Location.** Scholarships for people living in your community.
- **Citizenship.** Any scholarships only open to U.S. residents or citizens.
- **Extracurricular activities.** The more involved you are, the more scholarship opportunities.
- **Academic improvement/excellence.**
- **Area of study.** Scholarships for that particular field.
- **Excellence in sports.**
- **Excellence in other areas.** Music, art, drama, and so on.
- **Private agencies.**
- **Foundations.**
- **Corporations.**
- **Clubs.**
- **Fraternal and service organizations.**
- **Civic associations.**
- **Unions.**
- **Religious groups.**
- **Employers.** Some employers provide tuition reimbursement benefits for employees and/or the children of employees.
- **In-course or faculty scholarships.** Available after you are in a program.

Apply for as many scholarships as possible. A lot of free money is out there, and often it is left unused because students don't know about it or they think that they won't get it. No matter how unlikely you think it will be that you get the scholarship, if you meet the qualifications, *apply anyway.* The worst that could happen is that you don't get the money. The best thing is that you *do,* and that could mean anywhere from $100 to several thousands of dollars in free money for school.

Just Be Yourself

When filling out scholarships, you want to do just that: Just be yourself. Most scholarship money is given for who you are and who you hope to become. This activity is designed to come up with a statement of that.

You've just heard on the radio that your favorite music artist is coming to town. This person never goes on tour and is making a one-time appearance for a special charity event near you. Anyone is welcome to attend the event–as long as he or she pays the $100 donation for the ticket. The tickets will be on sale for only one day–this Saturday. You don't have a job and won't be able to find one in time to make $100, so you begin searching for other ways to come up with the money. No one is able to lend you the money, so you have to find some way to make $100 fast without breaking the law. You begin looking through the newspaper and find the following ad:

Immediate assistance needed: Looking for a few high school students to participate in a study. Students will be paid $150 cash to participate in a 2-hour focus group this Friday. In order to qualify, students must be in high school, be thinking about their future, be able to talk about goals they have, be involved either in school or the community, and be willing to communicate. If interested, please call (111) 222-3333 for further information.

When you call to find out more, you learn that you qualify for the focus group, depending on how you answer the following questions. If they accept you, you will be in the group and will earn the money you need to buy the tickets and a nice outfit as well. Look at the questions below and answer them as though you were trying to get into the focus group.

Write your answer to each question.

1. What year are you in school? _____

2. What do you plan to do after you graduate high school? _____

_____

_____

3. What activities are you involved in? _____

_____

_____

4. What do you see yourself doing in five years? _____

_____

_____

Now you may be asking, "What do these questions have to do with financial aid?" The answer? Everything! Think about this situation. In the preceding scenario, you were willing to do anything legal to get the money for this concert because it was something you really wanted to do. You stopped at nothing to come up with the money and you found a way to make it. You should see applying for scholarships in the same light. When you really understand the benefits of education, you should want to stop at nothing to find a way to get it. Scholarships and other funds are readily available for school; no one should use finances as a reason to not go to school. And, if you went through the preceding worksheet, you have the basic format for writing requests for many scholarships. Most scholarship applications ask similar questions as those listed above to see your motivation and that you are thinking about the future. The decision makers want to know that the money will be well spent.

If someone offered to pay all your expenses for college if you would write a letter that showed that you have a definite goal and the will to follow through, what would you write?

Request for a Scholarship

_____
_____
_____
_____
_____
_____
_____
_____
_____
_____
_____
_____

holla' zone: *a place for you to let out your thoughts*

imagine this: you and your friend are talking about the future during lunch. your friend would really like to go to college, but she doesn't know how she could afford it. she got her fafsa information back, and it looks like she's going to have to come up with $5,000 a year for school. she knows her parents can't afford that, and she doesn't know who else to ask. you mention scholarships to her, but she told you that she doesn't know where to find any and she figures she would probably never get any, so why bother. her face grew really sad during the conversation and her last comment was, "i guess i just can't go to college."

during study hall, you write your friend a note, trying to help her see the value of going to college. where could she go for information about scholarships? are there any other (legal) ways she could use to come up with the money for school? what would your note say? write a paragraph to your friend.

_____
_____
_____
_____
_____

What's It Take to Get into a School?

Regardless of the type of school you decide to attend, you must follow a process, taking certain steps to get in. Every school has specific requirements and deadlines; if you don't plan ahead, you may not get in. In this section, you learn about steps to take in order to get into a school.

Get Organized

In reality, school planning is not something that you should begin right before you graduate high school. The sooner you start thinking about education, the more successful you will be—not only in high school, but also in your future. The following activity lists different steps you need to take in to prepare yourself for going off to school. Try to see if you can put each step in the correct area on the calendar.

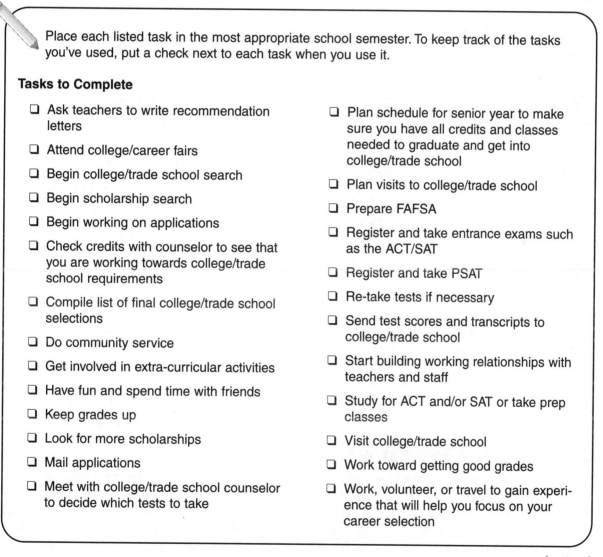

Place each listed task in the most appropriate school semester. To keep track of the tasks you've used, put a check next to each task when you use it.

Tasks to Complete

- ❏ Ask teachers to write recommendation letters
- ❏ Attend college/career fairs
- ❏ Begin college/trade school search
- ❏ Begin scholarship search
- ❏ Begin working on applications
- ❏ Check credits with counselor to see that you are working towards college/trade school requirements
- ❏ Compile list of final college/trade school selections
- ❏ Do community service
- ❏ Get involved in extra-curricular activities
- ❏ Have fun and spend time with friends
- ❏ Keep grades up
- ❏ Look for more scholarships
- ❏ Mail applications
- ❏ Meet with college/trade school counselor to decide which tests to take

- ❏ Plan schedule for senior year to make sure you have all credits and classes needed to graduate and get into college/trade school
- ❏ Plan visits to college/trade school
- ❏ Prepare FAFSA
- ❏ Register and take entrance exams such as the ACT/SAT
- ❏ Register and take PSAT
- ❏ Re-take tests if necessary
- ❏ Send test scores and transcripts to college/trade school
- ❏ Start building working relationships with teachers and staff
- ❏ Study for ACT and/or SAT or take prep classes
- ❏ Visit college/trade school
- ❏ Work toward getting good grades
- ❏ Work, volunteer, or travel to gain experience that will help you focus on your career selection

(continues)

(continued)

Pre-Junior Year	Fall Junior Year	Spring Junior Year
_____	_____	_____
_____	_____	_____
_____	_____	_____
_____	_____	_____
_____	_____	_____
_____	_____	_____
_____	_____	_____
_____	_____	_____

Pre-Senior Year	Fall Senior Year	Spring Senior Year
_____	_____	_____
_____	_____	_____
_____	_____	_____
_____	_____	_____
_____	_____	_____
_____	_____	_____
_____	_____	_____
_____	_____	_____
_____	_____	_____
_____	_____	_____

Take One Step at a Time

Whether you chose college, trade school, or some other type of training, the ideal time to begin planning for school is during your sophomore year. By this time, you should be at least thinking about whether you want to continue your education and what you may like to study, and trying to maintain your grades so that you have a better chance of getting into a school. But no matter where you are in school, it's never too late to begin planning for your schooling after high school. Take a look at the School Planning Calendar. Where are you in the planning process? What other steps do you need to take before you graduate? Answer the following questions for this section.

Write your answers to each question in the blanks.

1. What steps you have already taken to prepare for school? _____

   _____

   _____

2. What steps you still need to take? _____

   _____

   _____

3. When will you take action on each step? _____

   _____

   _____

4. What are some obstacles you have been facing in the planning process? _____

   _____

   _____

5. How can you work through the obstacles you are presented with, and who can help you?

   _____

   _____

holla' zone: *a place for you to let out your thoughts*

you might be thinking, "why do i have to start planning so early? i'm young. let me have my fun." you can have your fun, but be smart about it. planning ahead doesn't mean the end of life as you know it; it just means that you may need to rethink some of your decisions. you need to decide if the possible consequences of your actions will lead you to the place you want to be in the future—even those consequences that do not seem likely. if something negative were to happen, how badly would it hurt you and your future plans? think about some of the activities you are involved in right now. pick one and answer the following questions. (on your own time, you may want to do this for all the activities you are involved in.)

how does this activity contribute to your future goals? _____

   _____

   _____

(continues)

(continued)

> *how could your involvement either positively or negatively affect your future?* _____
>
> _____
>
> _____
>
> *how would you deal with any negative consequences that resulted from your involvement in this activity?* _____
>
> _____
>
> _____

How Can I Find the Perfect School for Me?

In order to find the school or program that is right for you, you have to not only know what schools look for, but also decided what you want in a program. As in a relationship, you may have to change some of your ways to get in, but you also don't want to sell out your core values just to get into a school that may not even be suitable for you. To help you learn more about this give-and-take process, go through the following section. In the end, it will help you find that perfect match.

Check Out the School's Expectations

Read this ad.

Okay. So what does that ad have to do with school? It looks like a classified ad. Well, you search for a school the same way you look for a job. To get accepted into school, you have to know what the school wants and meet those qualifications. As with searching for a job, if the school's offerings don't match your interests or you don't fit its criteria, it's probably not the school you want to go to. It is important to find out what each school requires for entrance and either prepare yourself to meet each require-ment, or rule that school out if you are not willing or able to provide what it looks for in a student.

Wanted: Future-oriented, conscientious individuals who are willing to work hard and become successful. We are looking for individuals who are motivated, have excellent people skills, and are good writers (or willing to improve their writing skills). Several openings available with a lot of room for advancement, great pay and benefits in the long run. Interested? Call us at (111) 222-3333.

Schools weigh a variety of factors when admitting students. The following are what schools look at in the admissions process. Next to each characteristic, write down information about you. This way, you know exactly where you stand when you begin your investigation.

Write your response in the blank provided, or circle Yes or No.

Criteria	Your Situation
Are you a resident in the state where the school is located?	Yes No
SAT or ACT (or other entrance exam) score	_____
High school GPA	_____
High school class rank	_____
Type of high school you attended (Public, private, college prep, magnet, alternative, other)	_____
Minority status	_____
Age of applicant	_____
Difficulty of high school courses (List Honors/advanced courses/programs)	_____
Extracurricular activities	_____
Community service and volunteer work	_____
Letters of recommendation (List teachers/counselors to ask)	_____ _____

If the preceding information leaves you on the border of the acceptance scale, you need to know that the following two criteria are very important in the school's final decision. Your responses in these areas can determine your acceptance, so they need to be strong.

Criteria	Your Response
Are you prepared for the interview with admissions counselor?	Yes No
Have you written your essay/personal statement?	Yes No

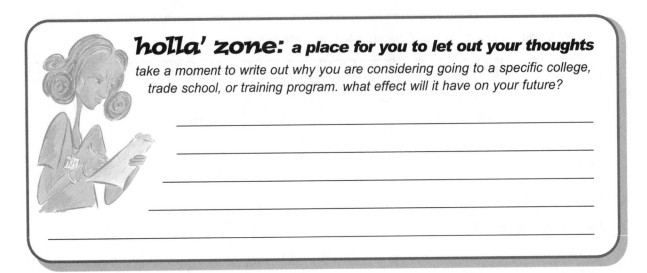

holla' zone: *a place for you to let out your thoughts*

take a moment to write out why you are considering going to a specific college, trade school, or training program. what effect will it have on your future?

_____

_____

_____

_____

_____

Admission used to be largely dependent on grades and test scores, but schools are now looking for a more well-rounded individual. If you do not have the grades but are involved in activities in your school and community, chances are you'll still get into the school of your choice.

I can hear you asking, "Is it too late for me?" No, you can do many things right now that will help improve your chances of getting in. You can join more extracurricular activities and community service projects today. You can work on improving your grades. You can get extra help from teachers and counselors on taking entrance exams. If you have already taken the entrance exams and done poorly, you can retake them. The second time you know what to expect. Start getting letters of recommendations. Get your English teacher or people who are good writers to help you with your personal essay. Think positive thoughts–it's never too late!

> *If you do not have the grades but are involved in activities in your school and community, chances are you'll still get into the school of your choice.*

Interview the School

After deciding whether you want to go to school and which type of school is best for you, you need to begin to look at specific schools. Books and counselors, as well as literature from schools, can all help you seek out schools that may fit your interests, but you have to know more about a school than what the brochure tells you. When you are making the decision about where you want to go to school, it is important to visit and "interview" the school. A school interview consists of not only asking questions to the recruiter but also checking out the campus.

For this activity, you are going to practice interviewing a school. It's best that you choose a school you are interested in attending, but it's not necessary. If you need help locating a school, look in the college resource center at the library. Use the following list of questions to ask and things to look out for on your school interview.

Write your answers in the lines.

Name of School _____

1. What type of school is this? (2-year, 4-year, trade school, career college, business college, other) _____

2. If this is a 4-year college, is it a teaching or research institution? _____

    ● Research institutes hire faculty to both research and teach students. Behind the scenes, though, the faculty knows that publishing is the primary priority of their job if they hope to advance and keep their job. So it may be hard to find these professors after class. Also, oftentimes, graduate students teach classes.

    ● Teaching universities teach general studies, have smaller classes, and the faculty is hired for their teaching ability. They have a better understanding for how various academic areas fit together.

3. What is the student/faculty ratio? _____

4. What are the most popular majors/programs at this school? _____
    _____

5. Is there campus housing available? If yes, what type? _____
    _____

6. What sort of financial assistance is available for students?_____
    _____

7. What type of assistance does the school provide students in preparing for job placement?
    _____

8. Where is most of the student population from in-state or all over the country? _____
    _____

9. May I have a copy of the student handbook? (This helps you to figure out if you fit into the school. Some schools have regulations and rules that others don't and if you don't agree with some of the rules, you probably shouldn't go to that school.) _____

10. Do you have a school newspaper, and can I subscribe to it in advance? _____
    _____

11. May I see a copy of your annual crime report? _____

12. What percentage of the faculty have doctorates and how many are alumni of the university? (It is not a good sign to have more than 20 percent of the faculty with their last degree coming from the same school where they teach.) _____
    _____

(continues)

(continued)

13. What religious groups meet on campus?_____
_____

Use this area to write down some of your own questions you have about this school.

_____

_____

_____

_____

Remember, you can use these questions only as a guide about what to ask. When doing a more formal interview, you should also formulate questions more pertinent to your specific situation, based on your likes and needs in order to ensure a best fit with a school. Take your typed (or neatly written) list with you. As you get answers, write them down. Doing so shows you are responsible and are capable of doing thorough research.

Explore the Campus

Talking to a recruiter is not the only means of finding out information about the school. Just as you go for a test-drive when buying a new car, you should always take the campus for a "test drive" to see whether the school provides the right learning environment for you. As you explore the campus, you may want to keep the following questions in the back of your mind.

1. Do students and faculty appear to be friendly?

2. Are buildings in decent condition? Does it seem as though the school tries to maintain the campus, or is it left in disrepair?

3. Do classroom buildings seem convenient to library, student union, and other sites of daily activity?

4. Where are dorms in relation to dining hall?

5. Does the typical classroom seating at the school suggest an average number of students or are most large lecture halls?

6. Does the library appear to be used for studying or is it like a lounge?

7. What sort of feeling do you get from the campus? Does it seem warm and inviting or do you feel out of place?

Remember, no matter how many questions you ask or how many times you visit the campus, you can never be quite sure if that school is right for you until you actually begin taking classes. When deciding on a school or program, make a decision that feels most appropriate for you, but be flexible.

If you begin attending a school but feel as though it isn't right for you after the first semester or two, don't be afraid to look into other schools. The purpose for going to school is to expand your knowledge and discover yourself. Before you change schools though, think through your decision very carefully and talk to others. There is no set timetable in discovering yourself. Some students adjust to a new situation immediately, and others take a year or two. If you really believe that you aren't getting the educational and social opportunities you expected, talk to a school counselor and look at the possibility of attending another school. Never forsake your education just because you feel stuck with a decision or in a school that isn't suitable for you. Whatever option you choose, don't abandon your search for a meaningful future. You may need to reexamine your dreams, but don't quit dreaming!

holla' zone: a place for you to let out your thoughts

whenever you're steppin' out to try something new, it's wise to get advice from someone who's been there. no matter where you are, a freshman in high school or getting ready to head off to school, there is always more information and advice that can help you prepare. so, find someone who's been there and ask them!

for this holla' zone, find someone who is going through, or has recently graduated from the same or similar program to what you want to attend. ask him or her for some tips on what you should and should not do to prepare yourself starting from the point you are. (if you don't know anyone personally, ask around or call a program near you and ask if they have students you could talk to.)

write the person's responses to your questions in the space below.

1. why did you choose this school/program? _____

_____

2. are you happy with your decision? _____

why or why not? _____

_____

3. what did you gain from your experience at this school?

_____

4. what are some suggestions you have for someone like me who is just beginning to look at schools/programs? _____

_____

5. is there anything you would have done differently? _____

_____

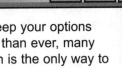

meta - Instant Message

no matter where you are on the school decision, it is always good to keep your options open and know that it is never too late to go back to school. now more than ever, many adults are returning to school because they realize having an education is the only way to advance in today's world. rather than have to look back and regret your decision, take time to truly consider the benefits of going to school and don't let any obstacle hold you back. there is always a way to make it happen if you really want it.

Got Skillz for Your Game?

Developing Skills for Success

I n this chapter, you will:

- Check out the benefits of patience
- Team up to get work done
- Set goals for future success
- Become a leader

Knowledge is a key to surviving in the world today. But, with all the advances in technology, what you know today is often out-dated by tomorrow. So how are you ever expected to keep up? Honestly, you can't. As an individual, you can't know everything about everything, or even everything about one subject, but with wisdom, patience, and an open mind, you can go much further in life. And, while each profession requires its own set of skills, some core skills will help you in any profession and many other areas of life as well. This chapter introduces you to these basic skills so that you can be exactly what you want to be.

Get to the point:

In order to get ahead in the world, you have to be patient, open-minded, and have some goals that you are working towards.

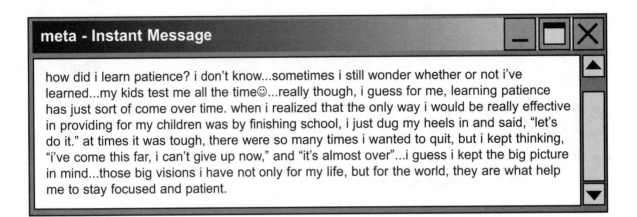

meta - Instant Message

how did i learn patience? i don't know...sometimes i still wonder whether or not i've learned...my kids test me all the time☺...really though, i guess for me, learning patience has just sort of come over time. when i realized that the only way i would be really effective in providing for my children was by finishing school, i just dug my heels in and said, "let's do it." at times it was tough, there were so many times i wanted to quit, but i kept thinking, "i've come this far, i can't give up now," and "it's almost over"...i guess i kept the big picture in mind...those big visions i have not only for my life, but for the world, they are what help me to stay focused and patient.

Just Chill Out and Learn Some Patience

The key to everything is patience! You get the chicken by hatching the egg, not by smashing it.

– Anonymous

Have you ever asked questions such as, "Why do I have to work for someone else? Why can't I just start out owning my own business?" Well, in order to run a business, you have to know what it takes to run a business. Working different jobs and going to school helps you learn the many different facets about owning a business. We can all be anything we want to be, but we need to go through a certain process and learn things before we can get to the top. To endure the process and the many steps involved in getting where you want to be, you must develop the skill of having patience, also called delayed gratification.

Often to get to the top you have to deny yourself of those things that maybe you'd like to have but aren't a necessity at this point in time. Yeah, maybe you'd fit in more with the in-crowd, but how far will they get you in life? After a certain point in life, it's not how you look that will get you to the top–it's your motivation and accomplishments. Waiting is not always easy, especially if you live in a situation where you've been struggling all your life, but if you can look for the bigger picture, it will be worth it in the end.

Choose Your Own Adventure

Sometimes it's not easy to see the big picture, especially when opportunities come up that seem to be quick solutions to problems. This activity will help you see that you have choices and that the first solution that comes to your mind may not be the best.

Read the following three adventures and decide which course you would choose. Afterward, read over the results to each action to see where you would end up.

Adventure 1: Let's do lunch

It's the start of a new week. Your mom just gave you $10 to buy school lunch for the week. You hate the school's lunches, but you eat them just to get some food in your body. As you walk into school, your best friend approaches you and tells you that a group of your friends are going to see the new movie release that is coming out this Friday and asks if you want to come along. You have been looking forward to seeing this movie and would really love to join them. You are about to say yes when you remembered that you just quit your job and don't have any money. Things are tight at home, so you know you can't ask your mom for any money either. Then you look down and see the money your mom gave you for lunch. What do you do?

❑ a. Say "No," and tell your friends that you can't afford it. You'll have to see the movie another time. You need the money for lunch; that is what it was given to you for.

❑ b. Say "Yes," and then skip school lunch all week and spend the $10 your mom gave you.

Adventure 2: Hook me up a ride

You are 17 years old. You live at home, go to school, and work. You have been taking public transportation everywhere, although occasionally you get a ride from a friend. You are tired of the bus, and winter is approaching. You can't imagine trudging through the snow one more year. You want a car. You have saved up some money, $700, and know of a friend who is selling his car. This car, though, is 10 years old and has some problems, but it runs. He is willing to sell it to you for $500, which leaves you with money to buy the title and car insurance for it. You tell your mom, and she suggests you wait to buy yourself a newer car, but you don't know if you want to. What do you decide?

❑ a. Take your mom's advice and wait to get a newer car.

❑ b. Buy your friend's car. You need one now!

Adventure 3: Promotion

You have been working at your job for almost a year now. You like it a lot, and it is really easy for you. Today, though, your supervisor approached you and asked if you wanted to take on a new position. You don't quite have all the skills for that position, and your hours would change. If you took the position, you would have to go to training, and the amount of work you would have to do would increase, but so would your pay. In fact, you would be making $4 more an hour than you currently make. You would really like a pay raise, but is it worth the extra effort? What do you do?

❑ a. Tell your supervisor you are not interested in the position. You don't feel you are the best person for the job since you don't have all the skills.

❑ b. You accept the position.

Results to Adventure 1: Let's do lunch

If you chose a., you said no, that you couldn't afford the movie. You skipped out on the movie so that you could eat lunch. Each day after lunch, though, you felt sick, and you were still hungry. By the time Friday night rolled around, you were left home alone because all of your friends went to the movie. You began wishing you hadn't spent your money on lunch so you could go with them. You even realized you could have made your own lunch, saved the money, and still gone to the movie. You realize lunch was not worth this loneliness.

If you chose b., you said yes, that you'd go to the movies: You realized that sacrificing school lunch for a week was well worth going to this movie. While you did have to wake up 10 minutes earlier to make your own lunch, you were out with all your friends and had a great time at the movie on Friday night. Not only was it was the best movie you had ever seen, but you also got to meet the star of the show, who happened to be in town and at that theater for the opening of the show. Life couldn't be any better!

Results to Adventure 2: Hook me up a ride

If you chose a., you decided that your mom was right. You really should wait to buy something more reliable. While you weren't excited to have to take the bus for another winter, you realized that even if you had bought the car, you probably would have ended up on the bus because of the type of work the car needed. Plus, you really couldn't afford to have had to take it to the shop every time it broke down. Guess what? One day as you were waiting for the bus, an old family friend passed by and noticed you. She stopped to talk, and you both discovered that she worked right by your school and her hours matched yours. She said she was willing to pick you up and drop you off at home or work every day. There were times you still had to take the bus, but not many. While you gave her gas money whenever she would take it from you, you were able to save even more money by not having to take the bus, so a year later you were able to get a car.

If you chose b., you decided that you just couldn't wait to have a car, so you bought the one your friend was willing to sell you. You spent all the money you saved up, but at least you didn't have to take the bus anymore, or so you thought. One evening, three weeks after buying the car, you were out with your friends when your car broke down. You called a tow truck, and with the help of your friends paid the $75 fee to get it to a shop. After the mechanic looked it over, he told you that your transmission was shot, and it would cost you $2,000 to fix! You couldn't believe it. That was more than what you paid for the car. You realized that it wasn't worth the money to fix it, so you sent it to the junkyard and made a few hundred bucks off it. Since that $200 was the only money you had, you couldn't afford another car, so you were stuck riding the bus that winter and the following.

Results to Adventure 3: Promotion

If you chose a., you decided you weren't the best candidate for the position, so you passed the opportunity up. You then discovered that the person who ended up in the position had less experience than you and soon became your supervisor. While your job remained the same, it became less tolerable because the person you were now working for managed your department poorly, causing more responsibility to fall on you. After three weeks of trying to help fix problems your new supervisor caused, you got frustrated and quit. After a month-long search for a new job, you found yourself in a similar position as before, with less pay. You couldn't find anything else because you didn't have all the skills companies needed.

If you chose b., you were a bit nervous, but you accepted the position anyway. You went through the training and found that you picked up on the new material fairly easily. Sometimes you had to do some outside research after you got off work, but after a few weeks, you were much happier with your position. Your supervisor was also very supportive in your transition, helping you and offering advice when needed. After two months in the new position, you found out your supervisor had promoted you because she was about to leave the company and wanted you to replace her. She noticed your dedication to your work and knew that you would be able to handle the new responsibilities. When she left, you were given her position and another raise. You then were making double what you were less than three months ago!

Wait for the Best

The previous activity provided some examples of how patience and sacrifice can pay off in the long run, but let's bring this concept a little closer to home and make it real for *you*.

Imagine this scenario: You're 16, a sophomore in high school. You live with your mom and brother. Life is pretty tough as your mom works hard, but there is still not enough money to get by. You have the clothes you have for school because the lady down the street found out your mom was having financial troubles, so she bought school clothes for your brother and you to help out. You hate not being able to have some of the things your other friends have…nice clothes, enough food, and maybe some of the latest music to listen to when you're riding the bus. One day a thought comes to you: You're 16. You can work! You don't have to live like this anymore. You could just quit school and work full-time. That way you would have your own money and could buy the things you need and help your mom out. But wait. Is that really a good idea? Let's think about this one.

Take a look at the following scenario for the breakdown:

Leave school and work now

> If you leave school at age 16, you can begin working full-time. Let's say you luck out and find a job paying $7.00 per hour. Each year you get a promotion and your pay increases to $9.00 per hour by the time you are 21. Your total wages are $18,720 a year. Because you work at this place for five years, you receive some seniority so your pay is decent, but if you lose this job, you may not be able to find another that pays as much.

> Over these five years, you will have made roughly $100,000. By this time, if you choose not to go back to school, you will probably hit a ceiling on your salary, so your wages will remain fairly constant for the rest of your career.

> By the time you reach 30 years of age, you will have made roughly $249,760, but you will have had little growth potential because of your lack of schooling. At 40, you will have made $436,960. You may have health insurance through your employer, but you may not have any retirement funds.

Now let's look at the other scenario.

Stay in school and go on to college

> If you stay in school, you can work part-time, so let's say you do that. As you are staying in school, you find some better paying jobs over the years, so although your hours are still low, you make a bit more money as you progress. Over these five years, you will have made roughly $43,000. This is working 20 hours for two years, and 15 hours a week for three years. (You will probably make a bit more as during summers you can work

full-time. I'm using a low-end number.) But, at this point, you graduate from college and decide not to go to graduate school. Your income opportunities greatly increase.

Let's say at the age of 22, you start making $27,000 per year. If your income increases only $1,000 each year, which is a low-end pay raise, by the age of 30, you will make $35,000 per year, so between the ages of 22-30, you will have made $279,000. By the time you reach 30, you will have made $322,000, and you still have plenty of room for growth, health insurance, and a retirement plan.

If, for some reason, your income never increases from this point on, by the time you reach 40, you will have made a total of $672,000.

Realistically, your income should increase more dramatically, depending on your profession, so these figures are very low. But they do show that, in the long run, it really doesn't pay to quit school. See the table below for a clearer picture of the breakdown.

AGE	QUIT SCHOOL TO GO TO WORK			STAY IN SCHOOL AND GO TO COLLEGE		
	Pay	**Hours per week**	**Yearly Wages**	**Pay**	**Hours per week**	**Yearly Wages**
16	$7.00/hr	40	$14,560	$7.00/hr	15	$5,460
18	$7.90/hr	40	$16,432	$7.90	15	$6,162
21	$9.00	40	$18,720	$9.50	20	$9,880
Total Income	$100,000 for the 5 years			$43,000 for the 5 years		
	Starting Wages	**Ending Wages**	**Total Income**	**Starting Wages**	**Ending Wages**	**Total Income**
22-30	$18,720	$18,720	$149,760	$27,000	$35,000	$279,000
31-40	$18,720	$18,720	$187,200	$35,000	$35,000	$350,000
Total Income	Between ages of 16-40, **$436,960**			Between the ages of 16-40, **$672,000**		

Now, use this worksheet to rethink your decision.

Write your answers to these questions:

1. What would you gain by leaving school early? _____

_____

2. Where would this decision get you in 10 years?

_____

3. What sort of job advancement and security would you have?_____

_____

4. How much farther ahead would you be? _____

_____

Now think about what would happen if you stayed in school.

1. What would you still have to do without? _____

_____

2. If you then went on to college, you'd have to give up things for four more years, but afterward, what sort of job would you have?_____

_____

3. What sort of advancement opportunities would be available?_____

_____

4. What would you be able to do with that income? _____

_____

5. How would you benefit by delaying a decision to work so that you could get more education?

_____

holla' zone: **a place for you to let out your thoughts**

*"To gain that which is worth having, it may be necessary
to lose everything else."*

– Bernadette Devlin

let's be real. when you're just barely living, wondering from one day to the next how you're going to eat or how the bills are going to be paid, it's not easy to hear someone say, "it's going to take some sacrifice." you're already living with next to nothing, and it's not easy going to school and living life seeing people dressed nicely, driving around in nice cars, talking about travels, and doing whatever it is that your heart longs for. you want your turn to be able to have those things. you know, it's not your fault you grew up where you did or that so-and-so did what he or she did to you. so why should you have to suffer; "those other people" didn't. well, you're right. it's not easy to sacrifice even longer when you already have very little.

(continues)

(continued)

for this holla' zone, write down all the "reasons" that come to you for why you "can't" wait any longer to make more money.

_____

_____

_____

then write some ways you can encourage yourself to stick with school or some other program that will help get you to the place you want to be in life.

_____

_____

_____

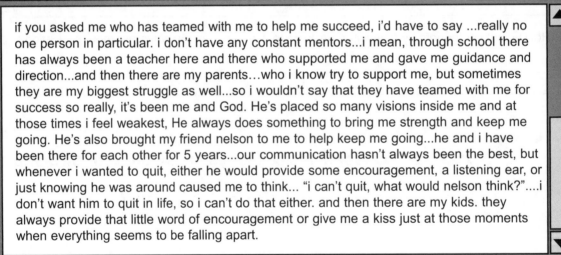

meta - Instant Message

if you asked me who has teamed with me to help me succeed, i'd have to say ...really no one person in particular. i don't have any constant mentors...i mean, through school there has always been a teacher here and there who supported me and gave me guidance and direction...and then there are my parents...who i know try to support me, but sometimes they are my biggest struggle as well...so i wouldn't say that they have teamed with me for success so really, it's been me and God. He's placed so many visions inside me and at those times i feel weakest, He always does something to bring me strength and keep me going. He's also brought my friend nelson to me to help keep me going...he and i have been there for each other for 5 years...our communication hasn't always been the best, but whenever i wanted to quit, either he would provide some encouragement, a listening ear, or just knowing he was around caused me to think... "i can't quit, what would nelson think?"....i don't want him to quit in life, so i can't do that either. and then there are my kids. they always provide that little word of encouragement or give me a kiss just at those moments when everything seems to be falling apart.

Teamwork: How Work Gets Done

In the world of work, we are given projects that need to be completed in a specific timeframe. Often, we do not have all the tools we need to accomplish those projects on our own, or at the best quality. The best way to accomplish the task then is working with others. This can be a problem in the workplace when people want to take all the credit or are unwilling to share ideas, but the results from teamwork are often much more effective and efficient in the long run.

Nowadays, companies are looking for employees who are skilled in teamwork, who know how to work on a team and share ideas and responsibilities. In this section, you learn more about the purposes for teamwork and develop your own teamwork skills. If you have trouble working with others, don't worry—you are not alone. There are others who will work with you on this!

Team Up: Two Heads Are Better Than One

No business can survive entirely by itself. It takes a variety of different staff members and often multiple businesses working together to get the job done. For each of the scenarios listed below, come up with as many different workers who would be needed to fulfill the job needing to be done. Each should have no less than six types of workers, so be creative. When you have thought of as many positions as you can, ask another person to help you and see if the two of you can come up with more. Put a star next to those that you came up with as a team. **T**ogether **E**veryone **A**chieves **M**ore!

Write your answers on the lines under the scenarios. When you've run out of ideas, brainstorm with someone else. Put a star by each answer that resulted from teamwork.

Scenario 1

You want to build a house. What types of work will you need done?

_____

_____

_____

_____

_____

Scenario 2

You are looking to start an after-school activity center in your community. What programs will need to be run and what sort of staff will be needed?

_____

_____

_____

_____

_____

(continues)

(continued)

Scenario 3

You want to start a restaurant of your own. What types of knowledge and staff will you need to hire?

_____

_____

_____

_____

_____

Scenario 4

You would like to be able to broadcast high school basketball on television. What do you need to do this?

_____

_____

_____

_____

_____

Scenario 5

You are looking to produce and sell your own CD. What types of skills and support will you need for this?

_____

_____

_____

_____

_____

Teamwork Builds Better Business

So, I bet you are thinking that work is just that…all work and no play. Well, you are wrong. Not all jobs work you to the bone and then expect you to be happy. In fact, many companies realize the importance of company "play time" in order to increase productivity, or the amount of work employees complete. So more and more companies are taking a few days out every year for staff retreats, a day where the workers come together, away from the office, and join in games and other fun activities to help learn more about each other and different departments, and brainstorm new ideas for how to work better back at the office.

Think about it. No matter what field you are in, if you want to build the best business, you have to have a staff that is effective, right? Obviously, the person who hired everyone knows many of the skills of each worker, but how does everyone else know about that person? They won't, unless they ask, which can be difficult to do on the job when everyone seems to be so busy doing their own work. Even though you may not have a job right now, think about how realistic this is for you. How much do you know about the others who are in your class? You may be sitting here, reading this and thinking about the type of work that you want to get into, wondering how you are going to actually be able to make it, and the person next to you may have a very similar goal and have access to resources that will help you get to that job you want. You will never know if you don't take the time to work with others and find out about them.

Role-Playing: A New Business Venture

For this activity, read the description of the company named Build UP. Then read the staff descriptions. All work for Build UP, but in different departments. The company is trying to come up with some new services that they can provide in order to increase business, but they don't want to hire anyone new right now. They figure they have enough skills in-house, that if they tap the right resources, they will be able to accomplish their goal. After going through each person's description, think of some sort of product or service that the company could offer that would use the skills of its employees.

Build UP is a small business that helps corporations improve company productivity, offering workshops, trainings, and seminars for individuals and groups in five states. Currently, Build UP offers workshops in team building, office communication, and group facilitation. Over the last five years, though, the folks at Build UP have noticed a decline in the quality of staff members within the corporations they work with. Many managers and executives are frustrated in the hiring process because finding quality employees seems to be getting more difficult. Build UP is looking for a way to help change this situation, which means expanding beyond just working with corporations and getting involved in communities themselves. The company just met with the mayor of the city and has been given approval to initiate a project that will help citizens improve effectiveness. The Build UP staff needs to come up with a program and community group that they want to work with—youth, senior citizens, or minority-run businesses, for example.

The company has the following staff members:

Eduardo is the computer technician. He has a degree in computer science, knows how to design Web pages, can fix any computer problem that pops up, and writes his own computer programs. Outside of work, Eduardo is involved in sports and nutrition. He is currently preparing for a marathon and is part of a basketball league. Additionally, he is married and has two small children, with whom he loves to spend time reading and playing games.

Shandra is the administrative assistant. She oversees all the billing and office communication and schedules all events for the company. On the side, she also invests in real estate with her husband. They buy old buildings, rehab them, and then sell them or rent them out. In addition, she is very active at a local shelter for abused children. She helps raise funds and coordinates events for the children.

(continues)

(continued)

Marlene is one of the trainers. She has a degree in Marketing and Business Management, has worked in sales and as a journalist, and has written two books. Personally, she is a single mother of a teenage boy who is very athletic, so she is very involved with his activities. Right now, she is working on a school committee trying to form activities for the kids to get involved in outside of school that will prepare them for the future.

Sean is another trainer. He has a degree in Psychology, has worked in sales, as a caseworker, and as a high school basketball coach. He is young and single, so he has a lot of free time outside of work. He loves to travel, play sports, and get involved in the community. He is very active in his church as well. Last month, he helped coordinate a mission trip to Bali, Indonesia, in which the group helped to rebuild a small village that was destroyed in a tropical storm.

Zaire is the Executive Director. He has a Master's degree in nonprofit management and a Bachelor's in Business Administration. He had worked in two of the top consulting firms before leaving and starting Build UP. He oversees all the administrative work at the organization. In addition to all the work he does at the office, he coordinates fundraisers for an organization that works with teen mothers.

Now that you have read more about the company and its staff, think of a new program that Build UP can develop. If you would like, team up with others from some more ideas. Use the following questions to guide you.

1. List the different skills/interests that this company has.

_____

_____

_____

_____

_____

2. What are some skills/interests that more than one person shares?

_____

_____

_____

_____

3. What are some ways these skills could be put to use on the job? _____

_____

_____

_____

4. What type of program could the staff develop? Who would the program be geared to? (Should the program be for a specific age group, career interest, organization, and so on.) _____

_____

_____

_____

_____

5. In the chart below, fill in each person's responsibilities be in the new program.

Staff Member	Responsibilities
Eduardo	
Shandra	
Marlene	
Sean	
Zaire	

Write a brief program description.

_____

_____

_____

_____

_____

holla' zone: *a place for you to let out your thoughts*

working on a team is not always easy. in fact, many people believe that they could do things much better on their own. for this entry, list what you see as some pros and cons to teamwork and then answer the questions following.

pros   cons

_____   _____

_____   _____

_____   _____

(continues)

(continued)

if you want, you can write more pros and cons on a separate piece of paper. then answer these questions:

1. *do you prefer working with others or alone?* _____

   why? _____

   _____

   _____

   _____

2. *how could teamwork help you in class or in a school activity, function, or sport?*

   _____

   _____

   _____

3. *what are other areas of your life that teamwork would make easier?*

   _____

   _____

   _____

---

meta - Instant Message

learning how to set goals…that's a tough one. i am still working on that. i mean, throughout my life, i have had dreams and goals in my heart, but rarely did i sit down and try to figure out all the steps i needed to take to reach those goals. i knew the major steps it took, such as when i began thinking about college, i looked at what it would cost, and began trying my hardest to save up enough money. then i looked at when i needed to apply, and always kept those dates in my mind when i was doing everything else. it's funny as i was putting this section together, i realized that i wasn't the best goal setter, but my skills are developing more and more. in fact, training for the marathon has really focused me more on setting goals. now, i'm reaching for the gold in the olympics, so i really have to do some serious goal setting.

Goals That Get You to the Top

If you plan on succeeding in life, you have to define your path. While you're not going to know every step from beginning to end, knowing how to set goals is a valuable skill that will help get you there. I know.

Goal setting is not the most exciting activity. Many people, including myself, have often asked, "Why do I need to set goals? I know what I want, so I'll just do it." While it is true that you can accomplish what you want without setting goals, I can make a strong case for writing down your goals and mapping out a process to getting them. The best support for this argument can be found in the following quotation:

"Write the vision, and make it plain upon the tables, that he may run that reads it."

This Biblical scripture provides understanding for why we need to set goals: Writing your goals down gives you a visual of what you plan to do, and in those times when you get discouraged and everything seems to fall apart, you can go back to what you've written, re-energize yourself, and continue in the race that is set before you. It is what will help you stay focused in those times when life seems to be throwing all it has in your face, trying to knock you off course.

Goal setting is an activity designed to assist people improve their lives. In order to be effective, though, you must set goals that line up with your vision and that you can reach. Some people set goals either too high or too low, and then see no change in their lives. You can avoid this frustration if you keep in mind some basic guidelines about goal setting. So, go through this section, read the guides and complete the activities, not because you are told to but rather do it with the expectancy of actually seeing your goals accomplished and your life changing.

The Lowdown on Goal Setting

Before you even begin setting some goals for yourself, you must understand the difference between goals and wishes.

>   *Goals* are desires that have action plans attached to them.
>
>   *Wishes* are things that people want but do not do anything to make that want a reality. They wish that thing would just come to them without having to do anything.
>
>   *Wishes can become goals* if action plans are behind the wish.

To make this clearer, let's look at this definition:

>   **Goal:** (*n*) A thing for which an effort is made; the place where the race ends.

So goals are the ending point of a specific race. The end is known from the beginning of the race, and an effort is made to get to that ending point. So, let's *goal!*

Before you begin, though, here are some final thoughts about goal setting:

When you set a goal, remember that it

- Needs to be challenging but realistically reachable
- Has to be quantifiable (you can measure or count it)
- Needs to have some sort of timeline

Here are some tips that will help you achieve your goals.

Tips for Setting Goals

- Find a quiet place with no distractions and take an honest look at yourself. Think how you can change your life for the better. Think about your goals.
- You need to understand why you want to achieve that goal. If there is no personal drive behind the goal, you are less likely to achieve it.
- Write goals down. This way you can go back to your goals and chart our progress.
- You can revise goals, but don't use that as a cop-out for not achieving them. If your situation dramatically changes, you may be wise to redefine or set a new schedule for your goals.
- Share your goals with others. If you don't, you are likely to not follow through.
- Revisit goals periodically to make sure you are staying on track. My recommendation: At least once a week.
- It is very important that you enjoy yourself in the pursuit of your goals.

Goals for Life

Goals can be set for all areas of your life. Look over the following seven basic life arenas listed below, and think of at least one goal that you can set for each area. You do not have to write how you are going to achieve that goal; just write a possible goal that you could set for yourself.

Write a goal on the line under each heading.

Mental Goal (well being of mind/emotions)	Family Goal (interacting with other people)	Physical Goal (health and nutrition)
_____	_____	_____
_____	_____	_____
_____	_____	_____

Spiritual Goal	Financial Goal	Social Goal	Career Goal
_____	_____	_____	_____
_____	_____	_____	_____
_____	_____	_____	_____

Stop for a moment and reflect on these goals. Are each of these goals designed to improve your life and the lives of others around you? Are these goals you want to accomplish for your life or what you believe you are "supposed" to accomplish? Remember: For a goal to be obtainable, it has to be something you desire to do. If you set a goal become a business owner because your parents want

> For a goal to be obtainable, it has to be something you desire to do.

you to stay in the family business, but you really want to become a teacher, either you won't fulfill your goal or you will be unhappy achieving your goal. Make sure that the goals you have for your life are ones that make you happy (and don't cause harm to others).

Practice Makes Perfect: Taking It Step by Step

When goal setting, you don't just set a goal and then go for it; that could get overwhelming. You need to take some time and write out the steps to get there. Breaking the big goal down into smaller steps makes it easier to accomplish the bigger picture.

To practice, make three goals for yourself. One goal should be able to be achieved within a week. The second goal should be achieved within three months. The third goal should be something that you would like to achieve in the next five years. Focus these goals on career/school related topics. On your own, you can make other personal goals, but for this project, please focus on this topic.

practice makes perfect

Goal 1: By _____, I will accomplish this career or school goal:
A Day Next Week

_____

1. What makes this goal challenging?_____

_____

2. What steps do I need to take to reach this goal? (List at least three things you need to do to accomplish this goal, new actions you have to put in place, such as give up something, talk to someone or get information.)

a. _____

b. _____

c. _____

(continues)

(continued)

practice makes perfect

3. How will I know when I have reached this goal? (What's my evidence?)

_____

4. Why do I want to accomplish this goal? _____

_____

5. How will this goal help me in life? _____

_____

Goal 2: By _____, I will accomplish this career or school goal:
<u>A Day Within Three Months</u>

_____

1. What makes this goal challenging? _____

_____

2. What steps do I need to take to reach this goal? (List at least three things.)

   a. _____

   b. _____

   c. _____

3. What can I start doing today to achieve this goal? _____

_____

4. What action can I take after I have completed the first step? _____

_____

5. What else can I do between now and three months to reach the goal? ___

_____

practice makes perfect

5. What else can I do between now and three months to reach the goal? ___

_____

6. How will I know when I have reached this goal? _____

_____

7. Why do I want to accomplish this goal? _____

_____

8. How will this goal help me in life? _____

_____

Goal 3: By _____ , I will accomplish this career or school goal:

        Your Age in Five Years

_____

1. What makes this goal challenging? _____

_____

2. What steps do I need to take to reach this goal? (List at least five things.)

   a. _____

   b. _____

   c. _____

   d. _____

   e. _____

3. What can I start doing today to achieve this goal?_____

_____

(continues)

(continued)

practice makes perfect

4. In one year, what are some steps I need to take to meet the goal?

    a. _____

    b. _____

5. What else should I accomplish within the first two years?

    a. _____

    b. _____

6. By the third year, what should I have accomplished?

    a. _____

    b. _____

7. By year four, what should I have accomplished?

    a. _____

    b. _____

8. How will I know when I have reached this goal? _____

    _____

9. Why do I want to accomplish this goal? _____

    _____

10. How will this goal help me in life? _____

Write your answers to the following questions.

1. Are your goals related to your future career plans, or are they based more on current needs that may have little impact on the big picture of your life? _____

_____

2. If your goals aren't related to your future career, could you revise them? (Remember: The object of a goal is to help you advance yourself, so you should not set a goal that is side-tracking you from what you want to do.) _____

_____

3. List any obstacles that you can foresee hindering you from reaching your goals.

_____

_____

_____

4. How can you either avoid those situations or work through those situations to accomplish your goal?

_____

5. How important is it for you to attain these goals? Why?

_____

Let Your Goals Be Your Guide

By now, you should be getting the idea; setting goals leads to a fulfilling life. While it's great just to hang out and chill for a while, when doing nothing becomes a habit and a large part of your day, life becomes boring. How is your situation ever going to change if you just sit in front of the TV, play video games, or kick it with your friends all day long? If you start developing yourself now by setting goals, you will have a happier life now and in the future.

Look at the three goals that you have listed for yourself in the previous activity and reflect on the career and educational plans you have for your life.

holla' zone: *a place for you to let out your thoughts*

goal setting is an important skill that you can use in every area of life. there is a saying that people move in the direction of their most dominant thought. so where you think, you will go. if you want to move up in life, set your goals high and keep focused on them. take this time to reflect on your goals, and write a paragraph about how you see these goals as helping you attain what you want for your life.

_____

_____

_____

_____

_____

keepin' it real

Josie knew that she always wanted to go to college. She had to pay her own way through school, so she aimed to do it as quickly as possible so that she could get her degree and then begin making a difference in the world. She set a goal to graduate within four years.

Early in her first year of school, though, Josie got pregnant. When trying to make decisions about what to do, she sat down and examined her goals. Her goal was to graduate within four years, but could she really do that with a baby? After much consideration, she decided she could. Although it was hard work, Josie set her mind to it. She worked out a plan so that she was able to care for her child and still make it through school.

At the beginning of her final year of school, everything seemed to be going well. Finances were tight, but the baby was happy and she was almost through. "Just one more year," she thought, "and it will be easier." Well, it *was* okay until she found out she was pregnant again, and the due date was two days before graduation! How on earth was she going to make it? At that point, she was working part-time, doing an internship, and going to school full-time. Her relationship with the father wasn't going well, and she knew she couldn't depend on him. The choice was tough, so Josie sat down again and reviewed her goal. Was it really possible to graduate in four years in her situation? She didn't know how she would do it, but she knew she couldn't give up now. She was almost there.

Despite all she went through, Josie stayed in the game. Things got real tough at times, but she pushed on. She worked things out with all her teachers and was able to finish her coursework on time. Two days before graduation, her baby was born. When the nurses told her she could stay in the hospital for two days, she told them, "No, I'm leaving tomorrow. I have to be at school the following morning to graduate." When her midwife heard the news, she came in and told Josie, "Go ahead. You deserve it." Not only did Josie accomplish her goal, but she was also able to attend her graduation with her two children by her side.

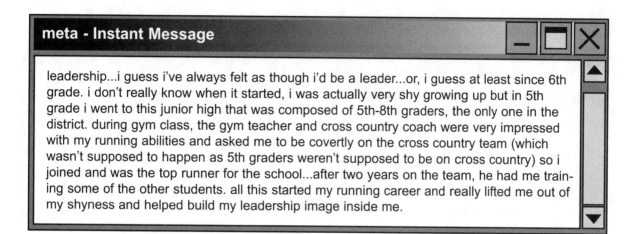

meta - Instant Message

leadership...i guess i've always felt as though i'd be a leader...or, i guess at least since 6th grade. i don't really know when it started, i was actually very shy growing up but in 5th grade i went to this junior high that was composed of 5th-8th graders, the only one in the district. during gym class, the gym teacher and cross country coach were very impressed with my running abilities and asked me to be covertly on the cross country team (which wasn't supposed to happen as 5th graders weren't supposed to be on cross country) so i joined and was the top runner for the school...after two years on the team, he had me training some of the other students. all this started my running career and really lifted me out of my shyness and helped build my leadership image inside me.

Leadership: Do You Have What It Takes?

When you are stepping into "the real world," schools and businesses often look for that special characteristic that sets you apart from the rest. It may be a bit nerve wracking to try to figure out how you can stand out, but it doesn't have to be. All it takes is some leadership skills, which is the result of improving your skills in patience, teamwork, and setting goals. Now you might be saying, "How am I supposed to develop leadership skills when I'm so young? Everyone tells me to just follow the rules. There's no leadership development in that!"

Guess what? That doesn't have to be anymore. I'm not suggesting that you stop following rules, but, in the right arena, you may be able to step out, propose something new, and make a difference in people's lives. Use the activities in this section to build those leadership skills not only to prepare for your future, but also to have an impact in your community.

Become a Leader

You may be thinking, "I am already a leader" or you may be thinking, "I don't want to be a leader." For some, being in a leadership role is exciting and fun, but to others it can be intimidating as it often has some big responsibilities added to it. Sometimes you don't have a choice; it just happens. Other times you can plan and prepare to be the leader.

Leadership can mean different things to different people, but it doesn't have to be as daunting as it may appear. The following are some examples of leadership roles:

- If you are the best athlete, your team counts on you to lead the team.
- If you are a natural at music or have taken music lessons, the band looks to you for direction.
- If you have had training and been working at a job for a period of time, new employees look to you for guidance.
- If you are the oldest at home and your parent leaves you alone with younger brothers or sisters, you are in charge.

Now think of your own situation and the leadership roles you have in your life.

Write your answers to the following questions.

1. Where are you currently taking a leadership role? _____

_____

2. How do you feel about this role? _____

_____

3. How can you use the responsibilities of this role in other areas of life? _____

_____

4. In what areas of your life can you improve your leadership skills? _____

_____

5. What are some areas in your life where can you step up and take more of a leadership role?

_____

6. How can you improve your role in these areas? _____

_____

Let's Get to Work

Leadership skills are vital to the workplace, especially for youth. Often, because of the lack of actual work experience, youth have trouble finding a job. It's that whole Catch-22; you can't get a job because you don't have experience, but you can't get experience without the job. So what do you do?

Well, if you have developed your leadership skills and know how to combat an employer's reluctance to hire you, you can score that job you were looking to get. Leaders are not people who don't know what they are doing; they are usually the ones who have been around a while, understand what is going on, and have ideas to help change or improve the situation. While you may have no actual experience in the job you're going into, if you can demonstrate assertiveness, knowledge, and desire to excel, the employer will sense that you have leadership potential and are a good candidate despite your age or any other issue that may be a barrier.

Think about the many issues that revolve around looking for a job and respond to the following questions.

1. What are some skills that employers look for when they are hiring? _____

_____

_____

_____

2. How can you use the skills that have been discussed in this section to find a job and be more effective on a job? _____

_____

_____

3. Some employers are afraid to hire youth, especially youth from lower income communities. Why do you think that is? _____

_____

_____

4. How can you personally demonstrate to employers that you have the skills necessary to be an effective worker? _____

_____

_____

5. What are some things you can do as a group to demonstrate that youth as a whole have the skills to work? _____

_____

_____

6. If you had the opportunity to sit down with a group of employers, what would you say to them about the employability of youth? (That is, what is it about what you have learned in these classes and other places that would make you an excellent employee to them?) _____

_____

_____

7. The issue of youth employment can be very controversial. As you know and can see in the above questions, some businesses, even though they may be able to, won't hire youth or don't pay them a fair wage. How can you take the lead and create a change in these attitudes? List some ideas here. _____

_____

_____

_____

Speak Up!

Some people are born to be leaders, others have to work at becoming one, but we all have the potential to be leaders in some area of life. The following paragraphs were written to stir up the leader in you. Read it and respond to the questions at the end.

People say that because you grew up in a certain neighborhood you're gonna be a certain way. Or, since your parents were a certain way, you're gonna do the same thing. Youth in general are often stereotyped and seen in a negative light, but what others think and say does not have to become a reality. It's hard when there are so many negative messages out there. Often times all you see in the media are kids in gangs getting killed and going to jail. Many times the media or other people's opinions of youth come to pass because we let them. Some young people figure, "Well, if that's what they think, I might as well be that way." They let society dictate who they become rather than becoming who they want to be.

With so many negative and mixed messages out there, it can be difficult to stand for what you believe in your heart to be true. What youth are often not taught and encouraged to do is to let their voice be heard. Instead they are told that they don't know any better and pushed to the side. As a result, some have turned to violence, drugs, and other destructive means to let their "voice be heard."

Listen Up! Just because you are young, does not mean you do not have a voice. Youth the future of this world. Your thoughts and ideas are needed to help change the many problems our world faces. Without your voices, how can anyone understand what is going on?

Adapted from Holler If You Hear Me *by Gregory Michie
(published by Teachers College Press, New York)*

Now stop for just one moment. Has this passage struck a cord? It should, and if it hasn't, then you ought to check yourself. Too many injustices are going on in the world today and too many people sitting idly by letting them continue. *YOU*th will be the ones to have to deal with the consequences. Now, maybe that will start you thinking. So take a moment and think of at least one issue that affects you, or youth in general, that you would like to see changed, and complete the questions. Use this exercise as a format to vent your ideas about the problems or what people perceive as problems in your community.

Take some time to really think about the following questions and then write your answers in the blank lines.

1. What issue really affects you or youth in general? _____

   _____

2. What are some messages you would like to send to others outside your community about this issue? _____

   _____

   _____

3. What can you do to get the message out? _____

   _____

   _____

Find a creative way to present your message, either by coming up with a campaign and then drawing a logo to represent it, or writing a poem, or lyrics to a song or a rap.

holla' zone: *a place for you to let out your thoughts*

while it's good to write down and talk about changes you want to see in the world, nothing will actually change if no one takes action. think about it. how often do you hear people complaining about the problems of the world? people sit for years, sometimes even their whole life, complaining about everything that is wrong, but do nothing to try to make things better. so i challenge you! take action and follow through on the above plans to create change. write about the results to your efforts.

_____

_____

_____

_____

_____

meta - Instant Message

this chapter provided just a touch of some of the skills you need to help you go further in life. remember, there is no specific formula, or quick route to getting where you want to be in life, but dedication and hard work will always pay off in the end. i always tell my students that, yeah, at times it's gonna get tough and you're gonna want to quit, but if you can stay focused and see the bigger picture—you know, your dreams—you can stay in the game. and one final tip, if you don't just think in terms of yourself but of how you can be an example for others, you may be a bit more willing to keep pressing on. use these skills you learned to take you to a new level in life now and in the future.

Where's the Best Game?

Finding the Job You Want

In this chapter, you will

- Discover your skills
- Learn what employers want
- Network for jobs
- Use the classified want ads
- Fill out effective job applications
- Learn to use the phone for your job search

Get to the point:

If you know what you're looking for and know how to get it, you should have a job in no time.

Finding a job is not as simple as saying, "I need a job. Please give me one." There are a variety of steps involved in the process and often if you don't follow the steps or proper procedure, you may wander around and lose out on that job. In order to begin searching for a job, you need to know

- What skills you have
- What type of job you want
- What employers want in job-seekers
- Where to look
- How to fill out the applications
- Proper phone techniques

This chapter walks you through each of these steps. Pay attention, though, because this chapter also gives you a key tool for finding jobs faster than usual.

Now it's time to get down to business. In the rest of the book, we're still going to have fun, but we're shifting into a more professional tone. In the game of life, there are different rules for different arenas. I made the language change you see in Chapters 4 through 6 to help you transition into the workplace.

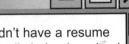

meta - Instant Message

i found my first job by going to the mall and asking for applications. i didn't have a resume then. i just filled out an application. i worked selling shoes (which eventually helped me land a job at their big downtown store during college).

i found the job i am currently at through a list serve that i am on. i have been very active in the puerto rican community, so i was put on an email list...through that list, i saw a posting for a job doing both program development and case management for youth. i was attracted to the job because it would allow me to both work directly with youth and give me the ability to design programs for youth, two necessities for any career i am involved in. i called to find more info, submitted my resume, went through 2 interviews, one was partially in spanish to test my language abilities (i hated that!), and then i was hired!

this job, though, is definitely not my end. in fact, it is just another stepping stone to getting to my real dreams—redeveloping communities all over the world. i want to get youth involved in development and policy making, providing housing for homeless youth, starting restaurants, and who knows what else. i do not plan on working for any organization for long. i want to be working on my own so that i can travel, spend time with my kids, and get them involved in my work without having to worry about what my boss might think. everything that i have done to this point is leading me in that direction.

Stop Wandering

Unfortunately, many people, youth especially, worry about finding a job because they may not have all the skills they need to get the job they want. Time and again, I have heard youth complain, "I can't find a job because I don't have the experience, but I don't understand how I can get experience without getting a job first." This is one of the most frustrating aspects of finding your first job, but don't be discouraged. There is hope.

Tap into Your Resources by Identifying Your Skills

The reality is that we all have skills; we just have to figure out what they are and how to apply them to the job we want. When it comes to identifying your skills, you may have to think beyond your actual work experience. Anything you are involved in utilizes some sort of skill, so think of any activities you are involved in and the skills you use.

The following activity will jog your memory to help you discover the skills you need to find a job. It lists just *some* activities that you may be involved in. Jot down others that come to mind as you go along.

Put a check mark next to each activity you've been involved in or add others to the list. Then, for each activity, write down the skills you gained. Do this for each category.

Various Odd Jobs	Skills You Gained in the Activity
❑ Running errands for friends or family	
❑ Taking care of siblings or other small children	
❑ Household chores	
❑ Repairing equipment	
❑ Cooking	
❑ Cleaning houses, cars, or pets	
❑ Pet sitting	
❑ Taking telephone messages	
❑ Managing money or budget	

(continues)

(continued)

School	Skills You Gained in the Activity
❑ Volunteering for neighborhood organizations	
❑ Yard work	
❑ Teaching younger children music or sports	
❑ Other _____	

Community Involvement at These Locations	Skills You Gained in the Activity
❑ Park district	
❑ Church	
❑ Community center	
❑ Block club	
❑ Other _____	

School	Skills You Gained in the Activity
❑ In the library	
❑ In the main office	
❑ As a teacher's aide	
❑ Tutoring other students	
❑ Volunteering at school functions, class projects	
❑ Holding a position on a team/club	
❑ Other _____	

Extracurricular Activities	Skills You Gained in the Activity
❑ Sports	
❑ Clubs	

(continues)

(continued)

Extracurricular Activities	Skills You Gained in the Activity
❑ Hobbies	
❑ Additional classes	
❑ Arts	
❑ Music	
❑ Theater	
❑ Other _____	

Read through the following list of skills. You can use these skills in most jobs. Check Yes if you have the skill, and No if you don't.

Area	Skills Built from Routine Activities	Yes	No
Budgeting	Do you get an allowance or have a job that enabled you to learn to budget your money properly?	❑	❑
Reception skills	Are you the one who always answers the phone and takes messages in your house?	❑	❑
Time management	Do you handle time between schoolwork, sports, school clubs, going out, and household duties well?	❑	❑
Event planning	Have you or are you good at planning parties, baby showers, and other events?	❑	❑

Area	Skills Built from Routine Activities	Yes	No
Health management	Do you have specific dietary/exercise routines?	❑	❑
	Do you help others stay in shape?	❑	❑
Supervising	Do you oversee little brothers and sisters?	❑	❑
	Are you in charge of making sure that everyone does the chores?	❑	❑

Take Stock of What You Have to Offer an Employer

Now that you have inventoried of all the activities you have been involved in, it's time to dissect each one and pull out the skills you have gained from each. Write down these skills in the appropriate category.

List your knowledge-based skills, those acquired from job experience and education. Examples: computer skills, analytical ability, and problem solving skills.

_____

_____

_____

_____

List your transferable skills, those you can use in any job. Examples: communication, planning, coordinating, follow-through, and leadership.

_____

_____

_____

_____

_____

_____

_____

_____

(continues)

(continued)

List your personal skills, those that reflect your personality. Examples: reliability, flexibility, sense of humor, ambition (these are the traits that cannot be taught by an employer). If you have trouble identifying these skills, you can ask people who have worked with you, or know you well, what they consider your strong skills.

_____

_____

_____

_____

_____

Use this information when you are looking at job ads to review the skills you have and help determine fields that you would be most qualified for.

When you begin the job search process, keep the following information in mind to help you find a job that fits your skills and makes you happy.

Tips for Work

- Compare all the skills you have with those the job requires. Emphasize the skills that the job requires. To make up for skills you don't have, show how your skills that were not requested can make you an asset to the company. If you present all your skills well, you can still get the job even if you lack some of the qualifications.

- An employer is looking for a variety of skills, but one of the most important is someone who has the right attitude. By selling some of your other traits and skills, you can overcome the fact that you do not have a great deal of actual job experience.

- Have a clear job objective. If you don't know what you want, it will be difficult to get a job.

- Be careful not to come across as desperate. Just because you need or want a job doesn't mean you have to give up everything else in your life. Employers should understand that you have school and family obligations. Most are willing to work with your schedules, provided you can realistically put in hours at the job and maintain your obligations. So, don't tell an employer you'll work whenever they want you to. Define your limitations.

- Know where and how to look for a job. Only 15 to 20 percent of available jobs are advertised in classified ads or on the Internet, and, of those 15 to 20 percent, half are filled by people who read the job description—the other half are filled by people who used networking or transferring. Sending resumes over the Internet or via the traditional method can cause you to miss about 75 percent of the jobs, so network! (Keep reading to find out how.)

- Follow up on all contacts. Most employers wait for you to call them to see how interested you really are in the position. If you haven't heard from someone in a week, follow up.

Understand What Employers Want

Now is the time to prepare to get the job you really want. To get a job, you must understand what employers want and what you have to offer. To prepare you for the job search, review the following lists. They contain skills and characteristics necessary in almost every job. Reviewing these lists will help you figure out what skills you presently have and which ones you need to obtain in order to get a job that suits you.

As you go through the list, circle the Y next to those skills you already have, a W next to those you are currently working on, and an S for those you will gain in the future.

Top Ten Personal Characteristics Employers Seek

Characteristics	Yes	Working on	Soon
Honesty/Integrity	Y	W	S
Communication Skills	Y	W	S
Flexibility	Y	W	S
Motivation/Initiative	Y	W	S
Self-confidence	Y	W	S
Interpersonal Skills	Y	W	S
Strong work ethic	Y	W	S
Leadership skills	Y	W	S
Teamwork skills	Y	W	S
Enthusiasm	Y	W	S

Skills Necessary in Any Job

Skills	Yes	Working on	Soon
Set priorities	Y	W	S
Retrieve info	Y	W	S
Interpret data	Y	W	S
Work with clients	Y	W	S
Manage people	Y	W	S
Diagnose problems	Y	W	S
Plan projects	Y	W	S
Make presentations	Y	W	S

(continues)

(continued)

Skills	Yes	Working on	Soon
Write reports	Y	W	S
Work with computers	Y	W	S
Work with technical equipment	Y	W	S
Set agendas	Y	W	S
Have work/internship experience	Y	W	S
Have academic or technical skills	Y	W	S
Show personal management skills (tardiness, absenteeism, lack of grooming skills, substance abuse, personal integrity, honesty)	Y	W	S

Get Smart

Nothing in all the world is more dangerous than sincere ignorance and conscientious stupidity.

– Martin Luther King, Jr.

Often employers ask or force youth to work under conditions or in positions that they should not work. To protect young employees, the United States Department of Labor has certain rules about how much and the type of work youth are allowed to do. If you don't know the laws, you may be caught in the grips of an unethical employer. This information may be of use to you. For more information, visit the Web site at

www.youthrules.dol.gov/jobs.htm.

When you	You can
Are 13 or younger	deliver newspapers
	work as a babysitter
	work as an actor or performer in motion pictures, television, theater, or radio
	work in a business solely owned or operated by your parents
	work on a farm owned or operated by your parents, but they can't hire you in manufacturing, mining, or any other occupation declared hazardous (listed below) by the Secretary of Labor

When you	You can
Are 14 or 15	work after 7 a.m. and until 7 p.m. except from June 1 through Labor Day, when you can work until 9 p.m
	work no more than:
	3 hours on a school day
	18 hours in a school week
	8 hours on a non-school day
	40 hours in non-school week
	work at these types of jobs
	amusement park
	baseball park
	gas service station
	grocery store
	movie theater
	office
	restaurant
	retail store
	not work at these types of jobs:
	communications or public utilities jobs
	construction or repair jobs
	driving a motor vehicle or helping a driver
	manufacturing and mining occupations
	power-driven machinery or hoisting apparatus other than typical office machines
	processing occupations
	public messenger jobs
	transporting of persons or property
	workrooms where products are manufactured, mined or processed
	warehousing and storage
	In addition, you may not work any other job or occupation declared hazardous by the Secretary of Labor (listed below).
Are 16 or older	work in any job or occupation that has not been declared hazardous by the Secretary of Labor.
	work any day, any time of day, and for any number of hours. There are no restrictions on the work hours of youth age 16 or older.
Turn 18	work any job for any number of hours. The child labor rules no longer apply to you.

According to the Secretary of Labor, until the age of 18, you may NOT work in any of the following hazardous occupations:

- Manufacturing and storing of explosives
- Driving a motor vehicle and being an outside helper on a motor vehicle
- Coal mining
- Logging and sawmilling
- Power-driven woodworking machines
- Exposure to radioactive substances
- Power-driven hoisting apparatus
- Power-driven metal-forming, punching, and shearing machines
- Mining, other than coal mining
- Meat packing or processing (including the use of power-driven meat slicing machines)
- Power-driven bakery machines
- Power-driven paper-product machines
- Manufacturing brick, tile, and related products
- Power-driven circular saws, band saws, and guillotine shears
- Wrecking, demolition, and ship-breaking operations
- Roofing operations
- Excavation operations

There are some exemptions for apprentice/student-learner programs in some of these hazardous occupations.

Don't Rush into Just Any Job!

Many people jump into the first job they find. Unfortunately, many of those people end up not liking the job and begin looking for another one very soon because they didn't

- do their homework
- find several employers to pick from
- look for an employer who best matches their needs and skills

Fortunately, you have now taken the time to identify your strengths and skills and what employers want. Now it's time to match your skills with the employers needs. The rest of this chapter provides you with the tools to find a job that will not only put your skills to use, but also be fun!

holla' zone: *a place for you to let out your thoughts*

so you may be lookin' at the worksheets you just completed like, "man, i really don't have any skillz. what am i gonna do for a j-o-b?" for starters, relax! you are still young, so you have time to work on this, and there is no time like the present, so let's get movin'.

take a minute and think about what you have learned up to this point. in chapter 1, you learned about volunteering and generating new ideas for following your dreams, so let's apply those lessons here.

for this holla' zone, come up with five things you can do in the next week that will help you gain some new skills. list these things here.

1. _____

2. _____

3. _____

4. _____

5. _____

now, write down what you think you will gain by doing the things you listed above.

_____

_____

_____

_____

_____

gold medal effort: if you choose to go the extra mile, after you have completed the activities you wrote about above, come back to this worksheet and write about what skills you gained and what you learned in the process.

_____

_____

_____

_____

_____

_____

_____

_____

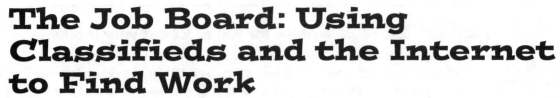

The Job Board: Using Classifieds and the Internet to Find Work

When searching for a job, old-fashioned classified ads or Internet are very popular options and can get you results. Using these methods requires some extra work on your part because you really have to have a good idea of what you are looking for and the skills you possess in order to stand out from the other candidates. In this section, you get some tips for using classified ads and the Internet, and work on job-seeking examples.

Help Wanted: Check the Paper

Classified ads are the most common means of looking for a job. Your local newspaper should carry ads on a daily basis. In addition, many cities have employment magazines, designed exclusively to post job ads, job trainings, and job fairs. These are all good sources to contact for job openings in your area.

Tips for Using the Newspaper Classified Ads

- Check out the newspaper each Sunday for the most recent job openings. Usually, the Wednesday paper has new ads, too.
- Many newspapers also list their classified ads online, so check the Web site. Sometimes newspapers post the ads online even before they appear in the paper.
- Most newspapers now have a separate career guide section, which contains useful job-hunting information.
- For more possibilities, look through classified ads from past weeks. Many times, these positions were advertised, but still not filled.
- Libraries are good resources because they usually have several newspapers to check out, they keep older copies of papers, and reading them is free.
- If you see job openings you like, try to call the person who supervises the position in addition to sending in your resume. Ask for an appointment to interview for the open position.

Role-Playing: Follow the Classified Ad

Following are examples of classified ads. Read through them and answer the questions to help your friend Jerome find a job.

Job 1

PART-TIME DEVELOPMENT ASSISTANT. The Art Design is accepting applications for data entry work, correspondence, reception. Computer skills essential. Flexible schedule. Salary: high teens. Send resume to: 333-422-1111/ myemail@emailme.com.
No calls.

Job 2

RETAIL Camping & Travel Outfitter is accepting applications for full- and part-time sales staff. Seeking enthusiastic, personable people with excellent communication skills. Outdoor adventure travel, backpacking or camping experience a plus. Retail experience preferred. Competitive pay, in-store discounts on gear, flexible hours, other benefits. Apply in person or fax resume to George, 333-444-5555. No phone calls please.

Job 3

PART-TIME RECEPTIONIST, $10/ hr. Exciting opportunity in a fun, fast-paced environment. Ideal candidate possesses high energy, great communication skills and computer knowledge. Responsibilities include answering phones, greeting visitors, and entering client data. Hours are Tues-Fri, 9-3. If you are a multitasker and would enjoy being part of a firm in a desirable atmosphere, call 333-777-0000, fax 333-777-0001 or e-mail theemail@emailjobs.com

Job 4

HOSTPERSONS AND SERVERS: Coco's Restaurant currently has positions available for full- and part-time host(esses) and full-time servers. You must have an outgoing personality and a sincere desire to make people happy. If you would like to be a part of the team that makes one of the busiest restaurants in the city successful, then come on down! Fine dining and high volume experience helpful for servers. Host(esses) need not have restaurant experience but must have high energy and an ability to be the life of the party. Apply in person, Monday-Friday, 3-5 pm, 222 East West Street.

Write your answers to the following questions.

1. Which job(s) can Jerome apply for if he has no work experience? _____

2. Which job(s) can he actually call to find out more information about? _____

3. To whom can Jerome speak to if he wants to find a job selling camping gear? _____

4. If Jerome is looking for a job in which he wouldn't be moving around all the time, which job should he apply for? _____

5. How can Jerome apply for that position? _____

_____

Searching WWW: The Wide World of Work

To expand your job search, try the Internet. Not only can you find classified ads posted on newspaper Web sites, but you also have access to a variety of job search Web sites. The Internet is a much more efficient way to find a job outside your state or country than any other method. Also, the Internet allows you to access company Web sites, which often have job postings that may not be listed in traditional classified ads.

Tips for Using the Internet

- The Internet is a great resource for searching for jobs and learning more about a company. If you don't have access to the Internet, try a school or the library.

- If you hear about a company where you might want to work, check out its Web site for more information. Often company Web sites provide information about their products and services as well as job openings. Employers believe that finding out about an opening through the company Web site is an expression of an interest in the company, not just an interest in finding a job.

- Web sites such as monster.com, careerbuilder.com, and hotjobs.com have many job openings for a variety of industries. Many people apply for each open position, so keep in mind that you may not get a response if you apply.

- The Internet also has Web sites where you can post your resume so that you can be noticed—even when you're not looking.

- If you apply for a position via the Internet, always be professional and never volunteer personal information.

Role-Playing: WWW.JobSeeker.Com

To better understand how to use the Internet for the job search, complete this role-playing activity.

> You've finally hit 16 and your mom's on your case—get a job or else. You decide to look for a part-time retail job in which you can work evenings and weekends because you are in school. The job has to be something you are qualified for (age, location, and type), so you figure you should look for an ad that states "no experience necessary."

Jump on the Internet and check out one of the Web sites listed below, or any other Web site that provides job postings. Search for a part-time retail job, and then fill out the following worksheet with information about one of the jobs you find. If you don't have Internet access, go to the classified section of the newspaper and search those ads.

www.careerbuilder.com   **www.hotjobs.com**

www.careers.yahoo.com   **www.monster.com**

Write your answers to the following questions, based on what you found on the Internet. Respond to all that apply. If a question does not apply, write NA.

1. What is the position/job title? _____

2. What is the name of the company? _____

3. Whom do you contact about the position? _____

4. What is the phone number for contacting the company? _____

5. What is the email address for contacting the company? _____

6. What is the address of the company? _____

7. Why does this job interest you? _____

8. What skills do you need for this job? _____

9. What shifts are they hiring for? _____

10. What is the pay? _____

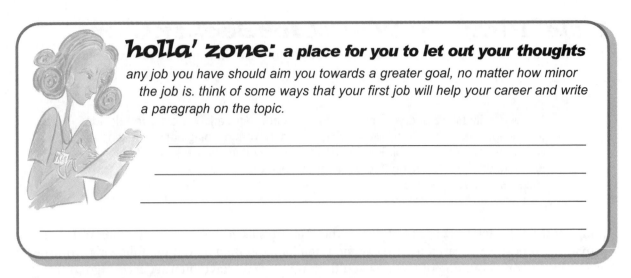

holla' zone: a place for you to let out your thoughts

any job you have should aim you towards a greater goal, no matter how minor the job is. think of some ways that your first job will help your career and write a paragraph on the topic.

_____

_____

_____

_____

Traditional Job Search Methods Just Don't Cut It Anymore

Before you read on, answer this question: "What is the best way to find a job?" Did you answer, "Submit a resume"? What about "Looking through the classifieds or going online"? Or did you say, "Go to businesses and fill out applications"? Guess what?!? None of these are right.

The most effective way to find a job is through networking. "What?", I can hear you saying. "I thought you said using the Internet wasn't effective." You're right, using the Internet isn't as effective, but networking is. Networking is not using the Internet. Networking is a process of talking to people in order to get something you may need or want. We'll go into this more in a minute, but let me just give you the lowdown on why tactics most people use for finding jobs aren't very helpful.

Studies show that an average of 245 resumes are received for *every interview* granted. (That's 245 for every interview, not position filled.) Four out of every five job openings aren't even advertised. Many times, though, these positions are filled faster than those that are.

Employers aim to hire employees that they feel they can trust and who stand out among the others. When you are applying for a position along with a pool of hundreds of other people, unless you have some superior qualifications or an "in" with someone in the company, you may just get lost in the crowd, despite how excellent of an employee you would make. Hence the need for networking! Want to find out more? Read on.

Networks Aren't Gifts; They're Built

What is networking? Of course, the *Webster's New World Dictionary* has definitions:

Network: Any systems of lines that cross: a group of people who work together informally to promote common goals.

Networking: The promotion of political goals or the exchange of ideas and information among people who share interests or causes.

Networking is a highly effective skill that people use to help them obtain information or other "things" they need, an act that involves communicating needs to another person in hopes that they may be able to assist either directly or indirectly. Networking can be a way to meet almost any need. In relation to the job search, networking is the most effective way to find a job (quickly!).

> *Tell anyone and everyone within two feet of you what you need, and you will eventually find what you've been looking for.*

To be able to network, you need to know the following information:

- What do I want?
- How do I tap into resources that will help me get there?
- How do I make myself valuable?

Let's look at each a little more closely.

What do I want?

> If you can't answer that, you can't network. You need to understand goals and form a solid plan. You should write down your specific goals (of what you want).

How do I tap into resources that will help me get there?

> After you set your goal, you must figure out the best way to achieve it, but don't expect to have all the answers. Networking is about asking people ways that it might be possible to reach the goal. Often you will find that how you think you will get what you needed isn't the way you end up getting it. Networking often leads you to shortcuts that make meeting your needs easier. Utilizing this "Two-Foot Rule" will help you network: Tell anyone and everyone within two feet of you what you need, and you will eventually find what you've been looking for.

> In the job hunt case, when you network, you don't ask only the people you think could give you a job, because that limits you and often ends up nowhere. You tell everyone you are looking for a job and ask if they know of any openings or if they know where you can go to find further assistance. Oftentimes people may not be able to give you a job personally, but they may know someone who could or someplace that is hiring. Sometimes, even if they don't know when you ask, they may remember you and come back to tell you when they do hear of something.

How do I make myself valuable?

> When networking, the other person is often asking what you can do for them as well. You need to be prepared for this and be able to present yourself in a way that makes you valuable to them.

> In the job hunt, people often aren't looking for you to actually do something in return for a lead, but rather they often want to know whether you are going to make them look good if they do refer you to someone for a job. If you are hired, are you going to be a good employee who will actually benefit the company? When someone refers you, your character reflects back on her or him. If you end up being a bad choice, the person who referred you will look bad as well, and no one wants that.

Everyone can network; people make the world go round. Even if you are the shy-type, just find your own personal style and you can do it. Don't try to be someone you are not–just so that you can network. Relax and remember these three important factors to make networking successful:

- **Honesty.** Always be honest about what you are looking for and why.
- **Good Judgment.** Assess the situation. If you notice that the timing is not right to ask, don't try to push the issue or you could make the situation worse. Also, if you meet someone who wants to provide you some assistance, but you have to do something illegal or that goes against your values, *don't do it!*
- **Trustworthiness.** Be true to your word: Don't promise something you won't follow through on. If you do, people will not want to help you in the future.

Building Networks

Let's practice networking. Following is a list of needs. Read over it and choose one need to complete this activity. Try choosing a need that you don't know how to get on your own. Then ask people you know to help you find what you need. Track the responses you are given on the worksheet. Remember: This is only an activity. You don't actually have to get the thing you choose. You only have to find someone who would be able to help you get it.

Choose one of the following needs by putting a check mark next to it.

❑ I need to get my car fixed, but don't have a lot of money. Do you know anyone who is cheap and reliable?

❑ I need help finding a babysitter for my baby sister this weekend so I can go to a concert. Do you know anyone who's available?

❑ I have this assignment for school and I need to interview a lawyer. Do you know whom I could speak with?

❑ I need money for college. Do you know of any scholarships or how I could find out about them?

❑ I'm thinking about becoming a vegetarian. What can I eat instead of meat and where can I buy it?

❑ I need to move and I'm looking for an apartment. Do you know of any available that are cheap and clean?

❑ I want to get something special for my girlfriend/boyfriend for her/his birthday. Do you know where I can find a store that customizes jewelry?

❑ I want to get some job experience by volunteering. Do you know where I could do that?

❑ I think I might want a career in politics? Do you know of a way that I can start learning more about that field?

Now answer the following questions, or circle Yes or No.

Person 1's Name: _____

1. Could he or she personally help you?   Yes   No

2. If yes, how? _____

   _____

3. If no, does the person know anyone or anything to help you?   Yes   No

4. If yes, who, what, or how? _____

   _____

Person 2's Name: _____

1. Could he or she personally help you?   Yes   No

2. If yes, how? _____

   _____

3. If no, does the person know anyone or anything to help you?   Yes   No

4. If yes, who, what, or how? _____

   _____

Person 3's Name: _____

1. Could he or she personally help you?   Yes   No

2. If yes, how? _____

   _____

3. If no, does the person know anyone or anything to help you?   Yes   No

4. If yes, who, what, or how? _____

   _____

Person 4's Name: _____

1. Could he or she personally help you?   Yes   No

2. If yes, how? _____

   _____

3. If no, does the person know anyone/anything to help you?   Yes   No

4. If yes, who, what, or how? _____

   _____

(continues)

Practice Makes Perfect: Nothing but Net(working)

Networking can be useful in all areas of life, not just in finding a job. Before you use networking to find a job, you want to make sure you really understand the concept. So let's do some more work on the topic. This time, let's make it personal. Find something that you actually have a need for.

For this activity, think of something you need but do not know exactly how to get.

1. Write your need in the bubble and then begin networking to find it.

2. On the lines stemming from the bubble, write down the names of the people you talked with and describe how they were able to help you. (Did they refer you to someone or someplace else? Did they have what you need?)

3. Don't stop after you fill all the lines. Stop when you get what you need.

Keep in mind that these 12 contacts can lead you to other contacts. You just have to ask for other contacts who may help lead you to your goal. Each line in the bubble may branch into another network or two. The more quality contacts you have, the better chance for a good job you have.

holla' zone: *a place for you to let out your thoughts*

as mentioned at the beginning of this section, in order to network you have to know a few things. one of those things is what you have to offer to the person you are networking with. for this holla' zone, read the following scenario and write your response.

you are looking for a job and you run into someone who has a connection to a job that would be perfect for you. you are so excited and ask if you can get the contact information when they tell you that they are allowed to refer only one person to the job. the employer is a good friend of your contact and said that whomever she referred would be hired. you are the second person your contact has come across who seemed like a good fit, so she has to choose who to refer. in order to make the best decision, she asks you the following question:

"i need to know that the person i refer is going to enhance the company. what can you say that will convince me you will do that?"

what is your response? use the following lines for your answer.

_____

_____

_____

_____

_____

_____

_____

_____

_____

_____

_____

_____

keepin' it real

Sandra had been working at her job on a university research project for almost two years. She loved the work, and everything was going well. Suddenly, the entire team was notified that, in three days, the project would be moving out of state and the employees would be out of a job. Sandra was shocked. She was a single mother with two small children and knew that she couldn't go a day without a job; she was their only support system. She knew that, with that short of notice, the likelihood of finding a job through the classified ads would be virtually impossible, so she got on the phone and email, and asked everyone she knew whether they knew of any openings. Within hours, she received a call from a former supervisor from her internship. The organization had just lost one of their employees. They hadn't even posted a job description about the opening. They immediately offered the position to Sandra since they knew her dedication and abilities in the field. Sandra was happy as she had found a job with an organization she enjoyed working in, and she didn't miss a day of work—despite the short notice.

On the other hand, Sandra's friend Jamie lost her job about six months later. She knew that it was going to happen and had some time to look. Jamie searched on the Internet, read through the classified ads, and applied wherever she saw hiring signs. Finally, four months after being out of work, Jamie found a job. She wasn't exactly happy with the job, but the pay was decent and it was work. That's all that mattered by this point.

While not the only way to find a job, networking generally proves to be a quicker method for job hunting and oftentimes results in a position you enjoy working in.

Filling Out the Paperwork

After you've found a company that is hiring, you've only just begun. There are several other steps in the process to being hired. And if you "miss it" in one step, you may ruin an opportunity to get a job you may have been perfect for. So, complete the following activities to strengthen your skills in the application process.

Bad Apps Culd Cost Ya

When filling out applications, there are some do's and don'ts. Rather than just reading through a list, why don't you try to figure out for yourself what you should and shouldn't do. Review the following application, circle all the mistakes, and count the number of mistakes you found.

APPLICATION FOR EMPLOYMENT

PERSONAL INFORMATION

DATE _1-02-0_   SOCIAL SECURITY NUMBER _420-16-8165_

NAME _Felicia   Jones_   AGE _21_
LAST   FIRST   MIDDLE

PRESENT ADDRESS _980 Madison   Chi   IL_   HOW LONG THERE? _7_
NO & STREET   CITY   STATE

PREVIOUS ADDRESS _123 Main   Chi   IL_   HOW LONG THERE? _10_
NO & STREET   CITY   STATE

PHONE NO. _511-1101_   OWN HOME _____ RENT _____ BOARD _____ DATE OF BIRTH _1-2-83_

HEIGHT _____ WEIGHT _____ MARRIED _____ SINGLE _X_ DIVORCED _____ SEPARATED _____   CITIZEN OF U. S. A.? _X_

NO. OF CHILDREN _____   DEPENDENTS· OTHER THAN WIFE OR CHILDREN _____   REFERRED BY _____

EDUCATION

NAME AND ADDRESS OF LAST SCHOOL ATTENDED _Riverside_   DATE _8-97 to 06-01_

CIRCLE LAST YEAR COMPLETED — GRADE 5 6 7 8   HIGH SCHOOL 1 2 3 (4)   OTHER 1 2 3 4

SPECIAL TRAINING AND SKILLS _____

MILITARY

BRANCH _____ FROM _____ TO _____ RANK _____ TYPE DISCHARGE _____ DRAFT CLASS _____

FORMER EMPLOYERS

LIST BELOW LAST FOUR EMPLOYERS, STARTING WITH <u>LAST</u> <u>ONE</u> <u>FIRST</u>.

DATE MONTH AND YEAR	NAME AND ADDRESS OF EMPLOYER	SALARY	POSITION	REASON FOR LEAVING
FROM 95 TO 97	Area Grocery	$5	Stock	Quit
FROM 98 TO 99	Star Garage	$6	Helper	Let go
FROM 99 TO NOW	Food Land	$7	Bagger	
FROM TO				

EVER DISCHARGED FROM A JOB? _____   MAY WE CALL YOUR PRESENT EMPLOYER? _____   EVER BONDED? _____

EVER ARRESTED? _____   IF SO, PLEASE EXPLAIN _____

PHYSICAL RECORD

HAVE YOU ANY DEFECTS IN HEARING? _No_   IN VISION? _No_   IN SPEECH? _No_

ANY OTHER PHYSICAL DEFECTS? _No_

WERE YOU EVER INJURED? _No_   GIVE DETAILS _____

IN CASE OF EMERGENCY NOTIFY _Patricia   Jones   980 Madison   511-1101_
NAME   ADDRESS   PHONE NO.

REFERENCES   EXCLUDING RELATIVES AND EMPLOYERS, GIVE THE NAMES OF THREE PERSONS YOU HAVE KNOWN AT LEAST ONE YEAR

NAME	ADDRESS	BUSINESS	YEARS ACQUAINTED
1. Eloise Estrada	982 Madison	Waitress	13
2. Jeffrey Jefferson		Cab driver	1
3. Patricia Jones		Secretary	23

APPLICANT'S AVAILABILITY

	MON.	TUES.	WED.	THURS.	FRI	SAT.	SUN.	HOURS ON OTHER JOB (IF APPLICABLE)
PART TIME ☒ DAY	ANY							_____
FULL TIME ☐ NIGHT								_____

AS A CONDITION OF MY APPLICATION AND/OR EMPLOYMENT, I AUTHORIZE INVESTIGATION OF ALL STATEMENTS CONTAINED IN THIS APPLICATION. I UNDERSTAND THAT MISREPRESENTATION OR OMISSION OF FACTS CALLED FOR IS JUST CAUSE FOR DISMISSAL IF HIRED. I AGREE TO FOLLOW THE RULES AND REGULATIONS OF HEALTH AND LEGAL AUTHORITIES AND SUCH RULES AND REGULATIONS THAT THE COMPANY OR ANY OF ITS LICENSEES MAY FROM TIME TO TIME PRESCRIBE, INCLUDING, IF NOT PROHIBITED BY LAW, LIE DETECTOR TESTS. MY REFUSAL TO COOPERATE WILL BE JUST CAUSE FOR DISMISSAL.

DATE _11-02-04_   SIGNATURE _Felicia Jones_

DO NOT WRITE BELOW THIS LINE

EMPLOYEE RECORD

NEW HIRE ☒   REHIRE ☐   WILL REPORT _____   HIRED BY _____

SIGNATURE – POSITION

IF REHIRE, GIVE DATE OF LAST TERMIATION _____

REMARKS _____
_____
_____
_____
_____
_____
_____

TERMINATION   MILIARY   FAMILY

DATE _____   QUIT ☐   REASON: TRANSFER ☐   RELOCATION ☐   DISSAT. ☐   SCHOOL ☐   OTHER ☐

PERFORMANCE SUMMARY

	EXC.	GOOD	FAIR	POOR
ATTENDANCE				
COMPATABILITY				
QUALITY OF WORK				
HONESTY				
INITIATIVE				
APPEARANCE				

DISCHARGED ☐

LEAVE OF ABSENCE ☐   LAYOFF ☐

ADEQUATE NOTICE GIVEN?   YES ☐   NO ☐

ELIGIBLE FOR REHIRE?   YES ☐   NO ☐

REMARKS (EXPLAIN TERMINATION FULLY) _____
_____
_____
_____

SIGNATURE - POSITION

Total number of errors found _____.

APPLICATION FOR EMPLOYMENT

PERSONAL INFORMATION

DATE 11-02-0   SOCIAL SECURITY NUMBER 420-16-8765

NAME Felicia Jones   AGE 21
LAST   FIRST   MIDDLE

PRESENT ADDRESS 980 Madison   Chi   IL   HOW LONG THERE? 7
NO & STREET   CITY   STATE

PREVIOUS ADDRESS 123 Main   Chi   IL   HOW LONG THERE? 10
NO & STREET   CITY   STATE

PHONE NO. 511-110/   OWN HOME ___   RENT ___   BOARD ___   DATE OF BIRTH 1-2-83

HEIGHT ___   WEIGHT ___   MARRIED ___   SINGLE X   DIVORCED ___   SEPARATED ___   CITIZEN OF U. S. A.? X

NO. OF CHILDREN ___   DEPENDENTS · OTHER THAN WIFE OR CHILDREN ___   REFERRED BY ___

EDUCATION

NAME AND ADDRESS OF LAST SCHOOL ATTENDED Riverside   DATE 8-97 to 06-01

CIRCLE LAST YEAR COMPLETED — GRADE 5 6 7 8   HIGH SCHOOL 1 2 3 (4)   OTHER 1 2 3 4

SPECIAL TRAINING AND SKILLS ___

MILITARY

BRANCH ___   FROM ___   TO ___   RANK ___   TYPE DISCHARGE ___   DRAFT CLASS ___

FORMER EMPLOYERS   LIST BELOW LAST FOUR EMPLOYERS, STARTING WITH <u>LAST</u> ONE <u>FIRST</u>.

DATE MONTH AND YEAR	NAME AND ADDRESS OF EMPLOYER	SALARY	POSITION	REASON FOR LEAVING
FROM 95 TO 97	Area Grocery	$5	Stock	Quit
FROM 98 TO 99	Star Garage	$6	Helper	Let go
FROM 99 TO NOW	Food Land	$7	Bagger	
FROM TO				

EVER DISCHARGED FROM A JOB? ___   MAY WE CALL YOUR PRESENT EMPLOYER? ___   EVER BONDED? ___

EVER ARRESTED? ___   IF SO, PLEASE EXPLAIN ___

PHYSICAL RECORD

HAVE YOU ANY DEFECTS IN HEARING? No   IN VISION? No   IN SPEECH? No

ANY OTHER PHYSICAL DEFECTS? No

WERE YOU EVER INJURED? No   GIVE DETAILS ___

IN CASE OF EMERGENCY NOTIFY Patricia Jones   980 Madison   511-110/
NAME   ADDRESS   PHONE NO.

REFERENCES   EXCLUDING RELATIVES AND EMPLOYERS, GIVE THE NAMES OF THREE PERSONS YOU HAVE KNOWN AT LEAST ONE YEAR

NAME	ADDRESS	BUSINESS	YEARS ACQUAINTED
1. Eloise Estrada	982 Madison	Waitress	13
2. Jeffrey Jefferson	(20)	Cab driver	1
3. Patricia Jones	(21)	Sectetary	23

APPLICANT'S AVAILABILITY

	MON.	TUES.	WED.	THURS.	FRI	SAT.	SUN.	HOURS ON OTHER JOB (IF APPLICABLE)
PART TIME X DAY		ANY		(22)				_____
FULL TIME ☐ NIGHT								_____

AS A CONDITION OF MY APPLICATION AND/OR EMPLOYMENT, I AUTHORIZE INVESTIGATION OF ALL STATEMENTS CONTAINED IN THIS APPLICATION. I UNDERSTAND THAT MISREPRESENTATION OR OMISSION OF FACTS CALLED FOR IS JUST CAUSE FOR DISMISSAL IF HIRED. I AGREE TO FOLLOW THE RULES AND REGULATIONS OF HEALTH AND LEGAL AUTHORITIES AND SUCH RULES AND REGULATIONS THAT THE COMPANY OR ANY OF ITS LICENSEES MAY FROM TIME TO TIME PRESCRIBE, INCLUDING, IF NOT PROHIBITED BY LAW, LIE DETECTOR TESTS. MY REFUSAL TO COOPERATE WILL BE JUST CAUSE FOR DISMISSAL.

DATE 11-02-04   SIGNATURE Felicia Jones

DO NOT WRITE BELOW THIS LINE

EMPLOYEE RECORD

NEW HIRE X (23) REHIRE ☐   WILL REPORT _____   HIRED BY _____
                                                                    SIGNATURE – POSITION

IF REHIRE, GIVE DATE OF LAST TERMIATION _____

REMARKS _____
_____
_____
_____
_____
_____

TERMINATION   MILIARY   FAMILY

DATE _____   QUIT ☐   REASON: TRANSFER ☐   RELOCATION ☐   DISSAT. ☐   SCHOOL ☐   OTHER ☐

PERFORMANCE SUMMARY

	EXC.	GOOD	FAIR	POOR
ATTENDANCE				
COMPATABILITY				
QUALITY OF WORK				
HONESTY				
INITIATIVE				
APPEARANCE				

DISCHARGED☐

ADEQUATE NOTICE GIVEN?   YES ☐   NO ☐

ELIGIBLE FOR REHIRE?   YES ☐   NO ☐

LEAVE OF ABSENCE ☐   LAYOFF ☐

REMARKS (EXPLAIN TERMINATION FULLY) _____
_____
_____
_____

_____
SIGNATURE - POSITION

What went wrong for Felicia Jones? Overall, the application is sloppy, which is frowned upon by employers. However, did you also find 23 specific mistakes? Look over the application and the comments to see which ones you missed and why each are considered mistakes.

1. Name written incorrectly (should be Jones Felicia)

2. Incomplete date

3. Social Security number is illegible

4. City and state should be spelled out

5. Needs to specify length of time: 7 what? Years, months, weeks, days?

6. Needs area code

7. Needs to check one of the lines

8. Write "Yes"

9. Not filled out

10. List entire name of school and address

11. Confusing dates

12. Not filled out, could put NA if applicable

13. Not filled out

14. Needs month and entire year

15. Needs addresses

16. Needs to specify whether the wage is hourly

17. Not completed for last job

18. Not filled out

19. Needs area code

20. Missing address

21. Reference is more than likely the mother or guardian of Ms. Jones. Relatives should not be listed.

22. Needs to fill out each box with specific hours

23. Should not fill out this section. (Read directions)

Bonus! Did you notice anything wrong in the application itself? An employer can't ask questions about

- Your housing arrangements
- Your marital status
- The number of children you have
- Your height and weight unless the information is required for the specific job
- Specific questions about disabilities

True or False: Completing Applications Takes Practice

To best fill out a job application, you have to have knowledge. This activity will help guide you in the right direction.

General Information for Applications

Circle True or False for each of these statements about completing applications. If the answer is false, change words in the sentence to make it true.

1.	Employers like to see neat handwriting on applications.	True	False
2.	If you don't have an answer, leave the blank empty.	True	False
3.	Put only true information.	True	False
4.	Fill out the application in pencil and then copy over it with pen in case you make a mistake.	True	False
5.	Abbreviate streets, states, name of company, and months to save time and space.	True	False
6.	Read only the parts of the application that apply to you. Don't waste your time with the rest of it.	True	False
7.	Turn in an application even if it has wrinkles or food stains. Employers will be grateful that you didn't waste paper by asking for another form.	True	False
8.	When listing dates, write out the entire year. (Example: 2001, not '01)	True	False
9.	You are required to answer questions about race, gender, or handicap status on an application.	True	False
10.	If you were never in the military, check "No" and leave section blank.	True	False

Personal Data

Circle True or False for each of these statements about completing applications. If the answer is false, rewrite the sentence to make it true.

1.	It is okay to write your nickname on your application.	True	False
2.	Put in area codes with phone number, but do not write the 1 at the beginning (Example: the 1 in 1-773-555-4444 is not needed)	True	False
3.	For "Position Applying For", write "open" or find out the specific position title.	True	False
4.	The best response for "Salary" is something higher that what they normally pay; you can negotiate down.	True	False
5.	The best response for when you can start is "now."	True	False

For the next four questions about various areas of the application, circle the letter of the best response.

Referral Source

1. What does "How did you hear about this job?" mean?

   a. What newspaper did you see the ad in?

   b. Who told you about the job?

   c. Who do you know that works here?

   d. How did you learn about the job opening?

Travel

2. The question "Can you travel?" means

   a. "Can you work at locations other than this one?"

   b. Do you take vacations?

   c. Do you have a car?

   d. Are you afraid of flying?

References

3. When choosing people to use as your references, (Circle all that apply):

   a. Use family members

   b. Write down former employers

   c. Choose people who have know you for over a year and who will able to give you a positive referral

   d. Make sure you notify these people first

   e. Use your best friend

4. Employer will contact these people and ask questions such as:

   a. Have you worked with this person before?

   b. Does this person have any kids?

   c. How does this person work in a team atmosphere?

   d. What is your general impression of this person?

   e. Will this person ever be late?

(continues)

(continued)

Work Schedules

In the next two sections, match the correct numbers and letters by writing a letter in the blank line.

Working Status	Number of Hours
_____ 1. Full-time	a. 10-20 hours/week
_____ 2. Part-time	b. Seasonal, as needed basis
_____ 3. Temporary	c. 40 hours/week

Shifts	Hours
_____ 1. Daytime	a. More than 40 hours per week
_____ 2. Nighttime	b. 4 p.m. to Midnight
_____ 3. Third shift	c. 8 a.m. to 4 p.m.
_____ 4. Overtime	d. Midnight to 8 a.m.

Special Skills and Qualifications

List some possible responses for the following categories:

1. Training_____

_____

2. Achievements _____

_____

3. Social/civic activities_____

_____

4. Computer skills_____

_____

Do you feel confident that you know all about filling out applications? Check out the answer section at the back of the book to see how you did. The answers to the last section about skills and qualifications vary.

Practice Makes Perfect: Fill Out an Application Please

Now that you know how, fill out an application for yourself.

APPLICATION FOR EMPLOYMENT

PERSONAL INFORMATION

DATE _____   SOCIAL SECURITY NUMBER _____

NAME _____ AGE _____
LAST   FIRST   MIDDLE

PRESENT ADDRESS _____ HOW LONG THERE? _____
No & Street   CITY   STATE

PREVIOUS ADDRESS _____ HOW LONG THERE? _____
No & Street   CITY   STATE

PHONE No. _____ OWN HOME _____ RENT _____ BOARD _____ DATE OF BIRTH _____

HEIGHT _____ WEIGHT _____ MARRIED _____ SINGLE _____ DIVORCED _____ SEPARATED _____ CITIZEN OF U. S. A.? _____

No. OF CHILDREN _____ DEPENDENTS OTHER THAN WIFE OR CHILDREN _____ REFERRED BY _____

EDUCATION

NAME AND ADDRESS OF LAST SCHOOL ATTENDED _____ DATE _____

CIRCLE LAST YEAR COMPLETED — GRADE 5 6 7 8   HIGH SCHOOL 1 2 3 4   OTHER 1 2 3 4

SPECIAL TRAINING AND SKILLS _____

MILITARY

BRANCH _____ FROM _____ TO _____ RANK _____ TYPE DISCHARGE _____ DRAFT CLASS _____

FORMER EMPLOYERS   LIST BELOW LAST FOUR EMPLOYERS, STARTING WITH <u>LAST ONE FIRST</u>.

DATE MONTH AND YEAR	NAME AND ADDRESS OF EMPLOYER	SALARY	POSITION	REASON FOR LEAVING
FROM / TO				
FROM / TO				
FROM / TO				
FROM / TO				

EVER DISCHARGED FROM A JOB? _____ MAY WE CALL YOUR PRESENT EMPLOYER? _____ EVER BONDED? _____

EVER ARRESTED? _____ IF SO, PLEASE EXPLAIN _____

PHYSICAL RECORD

HAVE YOU ANY DEFECTS IN HEARING? _____ IN VISION? _____ IN SPEECH? _____

ANY OTHER PHYSICAL DEFECTS? _____

WERE YOU EVER INJURED? _____ GIVE DETAILS _____

IN CASE OF EMERGENCY NOTIFY _____
NAME   ADDRESS   PHONE NO.

REFERENCES EXCLUDING RELATIVES AND EMPLOYERS, GIVE THE NAMES OF THREE PERSONS YOU HAVE KNOWN AT LEAST ONE YEAR

	NAME	ADDRESS	BUSINESS	YEARS ACQUAINTED
1.				
2.				
3.				

APPLICANT'S AVAILABILITY

		MON.	TUES.	WED.	THURS.	FRI	SAT.	SUN.	HOURS ON OTHER JOB (IF APPLICABLE)
PART TIME ☐	DAY								_____
FULL TIME ☐	NIGHT								_____

AS A CONDITION OF MY APPLICATION AND/OR EMPLOYMENT, I AUTHORIZE INVESTIGATION OF ALL STATEMENTS CONTAINED IN THIS APPLICATION. I UNDERSTAND THAT MISREPRESENTATION OR OMISSION OF FACTS CALLED FOR IS JUST CAUSE FOR DISMISSAL IF HIRED. I AGREE TO FOLLOW THE RULES AND REGULATIONS OF HEALTH AND LEGAL AUTHORITIES AND SUCH RULES AND REGULATIONS THAT THE COMPANY OR ANY OF ITS LICENSEES MAY FROM TIME TO TIME PRESCRIBE, INCLUDING, IF NOT PROHIBITED BY LAW, LIE DETECTOR TESTS. MY REFUSAL TO COOPERATE WILL BE JUST CAUSE FOR DISMISSAL.

DATE _____ SIGNATURE _____

DO NOT WRITE BELOW THIS LINE

EMPLOYEE RECORD

NEW HIRE ☐   REHIRE ☐   WILL REPORT _____   HIRED BY _____
                                                        SIGNATURE – POSITION

IF REHIRE, GIVE DATE OF LAST TERMIATION _____

REMARKS _____
_____
_____
_____
_____
_____
_____

TERMINATION   MILIARY   FAMILY

DATE _____ QUIT ☐   REASON: TRANSFER ☐ RELOCATION ☐ DISSAT. ☐ SCHOOL ☐ OTHER ☐

PERFORMANCE SUMMARY

	EXC.	GOOD	FAIR	POOR
ATTENDANCE				
COMPATABILITY				
QUALITY OF WORK				
HONESTY				
INITIATIVE				
APPEARANCE				

ADEQUATE NOTICE GIVEN?   YES ☐   NO ☐

DISCHARGED ☐

ELIGIBLE FOR REHIRE?   YES ☐   NO ☐

LEAVE OF ABSENCE ☐   LAYOFF ☐

REMARKS (EXPLAIN TERMINATION FULLY) _____
_____
_____
_____

_____
SIGNATURE - POSITION

BONUS! Since most job applications ask for the same information, you can use this application as a guide for when you go to fill out applications for a real job!

holla' zone: *a place for you to let out your thoughts*

a business reviews applications when it is hiring. so what are some ways you can find out to know which businesses are hiring? come up with at least 10 different ways to look for a job. be creative and see how many you can come up with. (hint: we discussed some of the ways in the beginning of the chapter.)

_____

_____

_____

_____

_____

Can You Talk the Talk?: Phone Etiquette for the Job Search

You know the saying, "You never get a second chance to make a first impression." Well, when most people say that in reference to the job search arena, they are generally referring to the interview. But, unless you've gone to a business with the intent of being hired, your "first impression" is often over the phone.

Many job recruiters can often pre-determine whether a person would make a good employee just by the person's attitude over the phone. Too often people are turned down for a job because of they lack professionalism in a phone conversation about a job. Fair or not, it's what happens. If you want a good job, you've got to play the game. The activities in this section will improve your skills.

But what if talking on the phone makes you nervous? You're not alone. Many people are nervous, especially if it is their first time looking for a job or calling a business for employment. We are often taught that we have to be perfect and know exactly what to say when dealing with a possible boss. These expectations often make people nervous and puts them in a worse position.

More than likely, you will not even talk to the boss when you schedule an interview. If you do, focus on the fact that this person is not a mean ogre out to make you look bad. An employer is often just as desperate as a job seeker–only he or she is looking for someone to fill a position. An employer who seems mean or frustrated may just be tired of interviewing "dead fish" and is about to give up hope. If you can come across as confident and sincerely interested in the job, you may be able to change the person's attitude so that he or she looks forward to your interview.

Role-Playing: Conduct Phone Interviews

Complete the next activity to get a feel for what the employer has to deal with when trying to find a new employee. This will help you put some of these pointers in perspective.

You are the owner of a cooking store. You've placed an ad in *The Local Town Paper* for a new sales associate. This position would be excellent for a high school student, as you are looking for a weekend and evening employee. You have been getting a lot of calls about the position, but you have only one opening. Read over the following phone conversations and see who might make the best employee, just by the response over the phone.

CALLER 1: SAM HOUSTON

You:	Good afternoon, Cooker's Delight. How may I help you?
Sam:	Um, well, I need a job and I see you're hiring, how can I get a job?
You:	In order to apply for the job, you need to come in, fill out an application, and meet with me for an interview. Before we set up an interview, though, may I ask how you heard about the opening?
Sam:	I don't remember. Some paper.
You:	The Local Town Paper?
Sam:	Yeah that's probably it.
You:	Let me ask you a few questions. What is your name?
Sam:	Sam Houston.
You:	Have you ever worked before?
Sam:	No, I'm only 17.
You:	What hours are you looking to work?
Sam:	I can work any evening, except Friday and Saturday. Also, I can work all day on Saturday and Sunday.
You:	I'll be doing interviews tomorrow between 2:00 p.m. and 7:00 p.m. When would be most convenient for you?
Sam:	I guess I could make it at 4:00. How do I get there?
You:	We're located at 124 South Main Street. Just off the corner of Main and Havanna. Do you know how to get here?
Sam:	Yeah, I know where it is, so I'll see you tomorrow at 4:00. Thanks.
You:	See you then. Have a nice day.

CALLER 2: MICHAEL PORTER

You:	Good afternoon, Cooker's Delight. How may I help you?
Michael:	Yes, I'm calling about the ad for the sales associate position that was listed in The Local Town Paper. Is the position still available?

You:	Yes, we are currently still accepting applications. In order to apply for the job, you will need to come in, fill out an application, and meet with me for an interview. Before we set up an interview, though, let me ask you a few questions. What is your name?
Michael:	My name is Michael Porter.
You:	Have you ever worked before?
Michael:	No, I am looking for my first job to help me so that I can go to college.
You:	What hours are you looking to work?
Michael:	I am flexible during the evenings on school days and Saturday's, but I cannot work Sunday because I go to church.
You:	Well, I'll be doing interviews tomorrow between 2:00 p.m. and 7:00 p.m. When would be most convenient for you?
Michael:	First, can I ask where you are located?
You:	We're located at 124 South Main Street. Just off the corner of Main and Havana. Do you know how to get here?
Michael:	Yes, I know where that is. In that case, I could make it there by 2:30. Will that work?
You:	Yes, that would be fine.
Michael:	Is there anything I should bring with me?
You:	If you have a resume, that would be fine. Other than that, just bring some identification.
Michael:	Okay. When I get there, where do I go and whom do I ask for?
You:	When you arrive, just come to the customer service desk and ask for Joe.
Michael:	Great. Let me just run the information by you again just to make sure I have it correct. You are located at 124 South Main Street, just off Main and Havana. So, tomorrow at 2:30, I will go to the customer service desk and ask for Joe. Correct?
You:	That's correct. I'll see you tomorrow
Michael:	Thank you. See you then. Have a nice day.

CALLER 3: YASMINE SANTA

You:	Good afternoon, Cooker's Delight. How may I help you?
Yasmine:	Hi, I'm calling for a job.
You:	May I ask where you heard about the opening?
Yasmine:	My mom told me about the ad in The Local Town Paper.
You:	In order to apply for the job, you need to come in, fill out an application, and meet with me for an interview. Before we set up an interview, though, may I ask your name?

(continues)

(continued)

Yasmine:	Yasmine.
You:	What is your last name, Yasmine.
Yasmine:	Santa. My name is Yasmine Santa.
You:	Have you ever worked before?
Yasmine:	No, but I need a job to help out my mom.
You:	What hours are you looking to work?
Yasmine:	I guess whenever—after school and on the weekends.
You:	Well, I'll be doing interviews tomorrow between 2:00 p.m. and 7:00 p.m. When would be most convenient for you?
Yasmine:	Well, where you are located?
You:	We're located at 124 South Main Street. Just off the corner of Main and Havana. Do you know how to get here?
Yasmine:	Yeah, I know where that is. How about 5:30?
You:	Yes, that would be fine.
Yasmine:	What am I supposed to bring with me?
You:	If you have a resume, that would be fine. Other than that, just bring some identification.
Yasmine:	Okay. Where do I go when I get there?
You:	When you arrive, just come to the customer service desk and ask for Joe.
Yasmine:	Okay. So, tomorrow at 5:30, I'll see Joe for an interview.
You:	That's correct. I'll see you tomorrow.
Yasmine:	Thank you. See you then.

Now that you have read all of the phone conversations, what do you think? Who would you hire, just based on what you heard? Answer the following questions to help guide your choice.

1. Who would you choose to hire? _____

2. What were some positive aspects about that person's conversation?_____

_____

3. What are some reasons you would not have selected the other two callers?_____

_____

4. Who would be your second choice? _____

5. What could this caller have done to improve his or her responses in the conversation?

_____

It is important that you get all the information you need for your interview while on the phone with an employer. This conversation helps prepare you for the actual interview. If you missed something, you could show up for the interview unprepared or late. Read the following tips to help better prepare you.

Tips for Scheduling an Interview over the Phone

- Make sure that you have paper and pencil in front of you before you pick up the phone.
- Write down the name of the person you will be interviewing with.
- Know where you found out about the job and the title of the job that you are inquiring about.
- Verify the information about the interview: Repeat the day and time of interview at the end of the conversation.
- Ask what sort of information you will need to bring with you.
- Thank the prospective employer for his or her time. It also doesn't hurt to tell the person you look forward to meeting him or her.
- Always take your resume with you when you go for the interview.
- If you have to cancel or be late (only in an extreme emergency should this happen), call the person as soon as you know that you will miss the appointment. If something happens that you cannot call before the interview begins, make sure you call as soon as possible afterwards and explain your situation. It may be possible to reschedule. (Don't wait several days later to call though.)

Answer Business Calls with Class

Sometime you aren't able to get in touch with the person who is hiring right away, or you are asked to leave your resume or application and told that the manager will call you back. In these instances, it is not only important to know what to say when you talk to the employer, but also it is crucial that your environment is prepared to handle calls about a job.

Answer the following questions to see how prepared you are for the job search process.

1. When an employer calls you and no one is available to take the call, is there an answering machine or voice mail that can take a message? _____

2. If so, what does the pre-recorded message sound like? Is it your favorite song, some funny message, or just a simple message stating no one is available so leave a message?

_____

3. When you pick up the phone, how do you respond? Do you say, "What's up?" What about "Yeah, what do you want?" Do you say, "Hello." _____

4. When you are on the phone, how do you talk? Loudly? Soft? Rapidly? At a normal tone and so that others can understand you?

_____

(continues)

(continued)

5. What aspects of talking to an employer over the phone make you nervous? _____

    _____

6. How comfortable are you with calling an employer to ask for an interview? _____

7. Are there any aspects of your phone etiquette that may need revising in order to enhance your ability of getting a job? _____

    _____

8. What are some ways to improve your communication techniques? _____

    _____

    _____

You may be young and it may be cool to have your songs on your voice mail, but when you start looking for a job, you have to remember that you are marketing yourself. Employers are looking for someone who will represent a company well. If you are serious about getting a job, there may be some things that need to change, at least until you find a job.

holla' zone: *a place for you to let out your thoughts*

so far we have talked about the necessity of proper phone "behavior." sometimes it sounds so complicated. all these rules and ways you have to be that just aren't you. what's the point? an interview! passing the "phone test" gets you into an interview for that job you want. with this in mind, let's keep looking forward. for this holla" zone, read the following excerpt and complete the activity.

have you heard the latest?!? the top recruiters from all industries are coming to town next. they're looking for only the best employees, which could be you! you don't want to miss this exciting event. in order to be admitted you must bring in a flyer highlighting all the reasons you should be hired. so be creative and come up with a personal advertisement that is sure to get you a job. remember: make some notes and write a couple of different ads about yourself. choose the best one. advertisements are short, so limit your final work to 50 words or less.

_____

_____

_____

_____

_____

_____
_____
_____
_____
_____
_____
_____
_____
_____
_____
_____
_____
_____
_____
_____
_____
_____
_____
_____
_____
_____
_____
_____
_____
_____
_____
_____

meta - Instant Message

the job search process can be a bit tedious at times and even discouraging. but following the guidelines in this chapter will put you on the right track to finding a job and give you an edge over others your age. remember, always walk into a job with confidence and direction, and even if you don't get the job, you will be remembered and looked upon more favorably.

How's Your Game Plan Look on Paper?

Writing Resumes, Cover Letters, and Thank-You Notes

In this chapter, you will:

- Write a resume
- Build your references
- Write cover letters and thank-you notes

So you've actually found a company that's hiring. Great! Now what are you going to do? You've still got to get hired, which usually means you have to be asked to interview, but you're not going to be asked for an interview just by sitting there; you have to show the employer what you're made of. You need to present your skills in a manner that is professional and shows that you mean serious business. This requires tools such as resumes, cover letters, and thank-you notes. Putting this information together takes a little time, but that time will pay off when you're asked to interview, offered a job that you really enjoy, and get paid nicely for it. If you've never done this type of paperwork, we've got work to do, so let's get going!

> **Get to the point:**
>
> In order to be noticed by an employer, you have to have the "write" stuff, and we're not talking about your looks. To find out how to develop your marketing tools—resumes, cover letters, and thank-you notes—keep reading.

```
┌─────────────────────────────────────────────────────────┬───────────┐
│ meta - Instant Message                                   │ _ □ X     │
├─────────────────────────────────────────────────────────┴───────────┤
```

okay, so I cheated. my dad actually put my first resume together. i don't remember if it was before my senior year in high school or at the end. i just remember the first time i really used a resume was when i was looking for a job during college. it didn't say much at the time, as i had only two jobs, but it has definitely grown from that point on. i have always saved my resume on a computer and disk, but there have been a few times that i have lost the electronic version, so i have had to re-create my resume. i don't like doing that...it's hard recalling all the different job titles and responsibilities. plus i've done so much that i forget about all of it until i pull out my resume, which makes it even more annoying when i have to re-write it. despite the downfalls of having to re-create it, my resume has been an excellent tool in helping me get jobs, scholarships, and into other opportunities so it's more of an asset to me than a burden.

Marketing Yourself: Building a Resume That Works

Before getting an interview, you actually have to be noticed by an employer. Yeah, sometimes you can walk into a business, ask about openings, and be interviewed on the spot, but these interviews are not very frequent. Generally, an employer wants to know a little about you so that he or she doesn't waste valuable time interviewing someone who's not even qualified for the position. So, in addition to an application, most employers ask potential employees to submit a resume. The following section helps you build an excellent resume, even if you've never had a job.

Resumes: Get Your Facts Straight

For some people, writing a resume sounds intimidating, but it's really just a simple tool that can land you a job in no time. Set aside your fears and see how easy it is to create a resume that's all about you! When you know the FAQs about resumes, writing one takes just a little thought and time.

What is a resume?

A resume is a summary of your skills and experiences. It is used as a marketing tool to enhance your chances of getting a job.

Who should have one?

Anyone who is or will be looking for a job should have one.

Where do you get the info to put on a resume?

To create a resume, select specific experiences from your past to show that you can perform well at the particular job you are applying for.

How long should my resume be?

At most, a resume is one to two pages. An employer gives about 10 seconds of his or her time to reading a resume. So be concise yet powerful—you have only 10 seconds to catch his or her attention.

Why should you have a resume?

- Employers ask for *resumes.*

- Resumes help to organize and detail your experiences efficiently so employers can easily reference them.

- Resumes leave some room for more creativity so that the employer can learn a bit about you before meeting you.

- Having an updated resume helps you recall past experiences when you fill out job applications.

BONUS! After you create a basic resume, you have little resume work to do in the future. If you save your resume on a disk and keep it updated any time you change jobs, join a new activity, or accomplish new skills, you really have to make only minor changes the next time someone asks you for a resume.

You should not use the exact same format of your resume for every position for which you apply. The most effective resumes are written for a specific job and refer to the requirements of the position posted. The more you know about the job you are seeking, the easier it is for you to tailor your resume to that position. If your resume demonstrates that you are qualified for that position, you are likely to be called for an interview.

> *The most effective resumes are written for a specific job and refer to the requirements of the position posted.*

Action Words Employers Look For on Resumes

Before you get caught up in how your resume looks, let's look at what the resume says. (Yes, you can choose from a variety of styles, but more on that later.) The most important role of the resume is to use the right words to demonstrate to the employer that your skills make you the best candidate. Following is a list of action verbs you can use when putting together a resume.

acted	debated	handled	met	recorded
adapted	defined	headed	modeled	recruited
administered	delegated	helped	motivated	reduced
advised	delivered	identified	negotiated	referred
analyzed	demonstrated	illustrated	observed	repaired
approved	designed	implemented	obtained	researched
arranged	detected	improved	offered	scheduled
assembled	developed	increased	operated	selected
assisted	directed	initiated	ordered	served
attained	documented	inspected	organized	serviced
brought	drove	instructed	originated	shaped
budgeted	edited	interpreted	oversaw	sold
built	eliminated	interviewed	painted	solved
calculated	enforced	invented	participated	spoke
cared for	established	investigated	perceived	studied
changed	evaluated	judged	performed	summarized
checked	examined	kept	persevered	supervised
coached	expanded	learned	photographed	supplied
collected	experimented	lectured	piloted	taught
communicated	facilitated	led	planned	trained
compared	filed	lifted	presented	tutored
completed	financed	listened	promoted	typed
computed	fixed	logged	publicized	unified
coordinated	followed	made	purchased	upgraded
copied	fostered	maintained	questioned	utilized
counseled	founded	managed	read	verbalized
counted	gathered	manipulated	reasoned	weighted
created	gave	mediated	received	wrote
dealt	governed	memorized	recommended	
decided	guided	mentored	reconciled	

Here are two examples of phrases that have action verbs and can be used in a resume:

> <u>Tutored</u> elementary school children

> <u>Read</u> books to children

Learn from Examples

You get a chance to build your resume in this section. Before you begin, however, look at the "Tap into Your Resources by Identifying Your Skills" section in Chapter 4 to review the skills that you can add to your own resume. Then read through the following guidelines, review the sample resumes, and choose the format you prefer for your own resume.

Sample resumes

Tonya Williams
4886 School Drive
Chicago, Illinois 67896
(345) 655-7654
tonya1@email.com

Objective
To obtain a position as a sales associate in order to enhance my customer service skills

Education
Gordan High School
Chicago, Illinois
Graduation: June 2002

Experience
Hostess   **June 2001-September 2002**
Yummy Restaurant
Chicago, Illinois
Assisted customers
Answered phones
Oversaw cash register

Babysitter   **March 1998- May 2001**
Supervised up to four children
Prepared meals
Created structured activities
Changed diapers

Volunteerism
Tutor   **January 2001-March 2002**
Assisted peers with homework
in various subjects

Skills
Computer skills
Microsoft Word, Excel, PowerPoint, Outlook, Internet

Leadership skills
Captain of the high school basketball team   2001- 2002
Secretary of the senior class   2001- 2002
Student council   2001- 2002

Orlando Cruz
994 Home Street
Los Angeles, California 90004
(223)355-4555
Olan1@email.com

Education: California High School
              Expected Graduation: June 2005
              Major: Theatre Design/Production
              GPA: 3.92/4.0

Work Experience:
6/2003 – Present   United Airlines, Los Angeles International Airport, Los Angeles,
California

Unaccompanied Minor Runner: Responsibilities include assisting
unaccompanied children to connecting flights within airport, assisting in the
coordination of task assignments in the Unaccompanied Minor (UM) Center,
assisting in the training of new UM Runners, customer service, and
maintaining a clean and healthy environment for the children.

Extracurricular Activities:
California High School Theatre
LA Rock Climbing Club
Community Service Committee at LA Community Center

Special Interests/Skills:
Travel
Fluent in Spanish
Rock Climbing
Technical Theatre

Honors and Awards:
Honor Student
Community Service Scholar Award

JENNY CROSS

123 Main Street   jenny1@email.com
Rochester, New York 23456   (555) 766-7766

Objective

To secure a position utilizing my customer service training and experience in the field of retail.

Profile

- Outstanding leadership and supervisory skills
- Excellent communication, and computer skills
- Detail oriented, well organized, and skilled in setting priorities
- Highly resourceful, critical thinker, and proven problem solver

Career Overview

- Special Events and Activity Coordinator
- Group Facilitation
- Crisis Intervention
- Team Leadership

Highlights of Experience

- President of sophomore and junior classes
- Coordinated student campaign to stop gang violence in my community
- Captain of girl's softball team, 2 years
- Recognized by peers and mentors for outstanding presentation and leadership style

Employment History

Customer Service Associate, Women's Retail, January 2003-Present

Child care provider, private families, October, 1999-Present

Computer Skills

- Microsoft Word
- Microsoft Excel
- Internet

Education

Grandville High School: graduated June, 2005

No matter what style of resume you use, follow these guidelines for a more effective end product.

Tips for Creating a Resume

- Keep it short—one or two pages max.

- Don't use sentences, just short phrases.

- Use action verbs to describe job responsibilities.

- Never abbreviate.

- Avoid jargon and technical words.

- Make sure to proofread.

- Use present verb tense for your current job (Example: <u>Tutor</u> children) and past tense for past jobs (Example: <u>Tutored</u> children).

- Market yourself (in other words, focus on your strengths and achievements).

- Emphasize experience in area related to job, de-emphasize experiences that are irrelevant (not related to the job).

- Don't include pictures unless you are applying for something like acting or modeling.

- List education first if you are a recent graduate.

- Never include your GPA if it is less than 3.0 on a 4.0 scale.

- Writing "References available upon request" is unnecessary.

Practice Makes Perfect: Resume for Work Experience

This section has two blank resume templates. The first is helpful for those who have worked; the second is for anyone, but especially for those who have never worked. With these examples to guide you, you can easily type your resume on a computer and then save it to a disk for future use.

The following resume format is best for those who have past work experience. If that's you, complete this blank resume with your personal information. You can then type it on a computer, saving it into an electronic format. If you don't have previous work experience, keep reading.

Work Experience Version of Resume

practice makes perfect

_____
Write your name on the line above

_____
Write your address

_____
Write your city, state, and zip code

_____
Write your phone number

_____
Write your e-mail address

Objective

_____
Briefly describe the intent of the resume. What type of position are you looking for?

Education

_____
Write the name of your school

_____
Write the address, city, and state of your school

_____   _____
Write your major (if applicable)   Write your graduation month and year

Experience

_____   _____
Write the title of your most recent   Write the dates of your employment

_____
Write the name of the place of your employment

_____
Write the address, city, and state of the place of your employment
List all your duties below:

_____   _____

_____   _____

_____   _____

_____   _____
Write the title of your most recent job   Write the dates of your employment

_____
Write the name of the place of your employment

_____
Write the address, city, and state of the place of your employment
List all your duties below:

_____   _____

_____   _____

_____   _____

Practice Makes Perfect: Resume for No Work Experience

If you don't have any paid work experience, you can still put together a resume. Employers will be impressed by your initiative. Complete the following worksheet with your personal information.

practice makes perfect

No Work Experience Version of Resume

Name_____

ADDRESS: _____

PHONE: (   ) _____   EMAIL:_____

Objective

Write objective:_____

Profile

- Brief point about self _____
- Brief point about self _____
- Brief point about self _____

Highlights of Experience

- State activities involved in: _____
- List any positions of leadership: _____
- State activities involved in: _____
- List any positions of leadership: _____
- Mention any achievements: _____

Employment/Volunteer History

Title: _____   Location: _____Dates: _____

Title: _____   Location: _____Dates: _____

Computer Skills (List all programs you can use)

_____   _____

_____   _____

_____   _____

Education

Name of School _____   Graduation Date _____

Check Your References

Most employers will eventually ask for some references so that they can verify your work ethic. Putting this information together is easiest while you are creating your resume because you are already in the groove of recalling past work and volunteer experiences, so it should be easy to come up with a few names and phone numbers as well. (You also reviewed this information in Chapter 4, so check back there to jog your memory.) Although you are putting this reference sheet together at the same time as you are doing your resume, you shouldn't hand it out until the employer has met with you and asks for it. The employer should get to know you personally before calling anyone to check up on you. To get an idea for what a reference sheet looks like, check out this sample before you make your own reference page.

References
for
Rosa Jimenez

Ms. Alba Parks, Supervisor
Parks Community Organization
(345) 234-5678

Mr. Victor Ortega,
Program Coordinator
YMCA
(345) 567-7890

Ms. Zelia Owens, Teacher
Parks High School
(345) 345-4567

Read over the tips for references, and you'll feel totally prepared for creating your own list of references.

Tips for References

- First, ask people if you can use their names as references.
- Use people you have known for more than one year.
- List people who will say good things about you.
- Do not use family members' names as references.
- Give a phone number where the person can be reached during the day.

(continues)

(continued)

- List at least three people from the following sources:

Teacher	Job coach	Community leader
Coach	Older co-worker	Supervisor from past job or volunteer experience
School counselor	Church leader	

- Don't submit references until they're requested.

Practice Makes Perfect: Reference-Building Worksheet

To create your own references, answer the following questions, and then go to your resume file on the computer and create your reference page in a separate file.

practice makes perfect

Reference 1

What is the person's name? _____

What is his/her position/title? _____

How do you know him/her? _____

Where does he/she work? _____

What is the area code and daytime phone number for this person? (____) _____

Reference 2

What is the person's name? _____

What is his/her position/title? _____

How do you know him/her? _____

Where does he/she work? _____

What is the area code and daytime phone number for this person? (____) _____

Reference 3

What is the person's name? _____

What is his/her position/title? _____

How do you know him/her? _____

Where does he/she work? _____

What is the area code and daytime phone number for this person? (____) _____

holla' zone: a place for you to let out your thoughts

think about your resume and the experiences of your life. pick one experience that was most interesting to you and write at least 2 paragraphs (at least 7 sentences in each paragraph) about it. the first paragraph should discuss the experience and the second should talk about how the experience has impacted you and your plans for your future. in your writing, address the following questions.

what was this activity? _____

where did it take place? _____

how old were you? _____

what were the most interesting/exciting aspects of this experience? _____

what aspects of this experience would help you in the workplace? _____

_____
_____
_____
_____
_____
_____
_____
_____
_____
_____
_____
_____
_____
_____
_____
_____
_____
_____

What to Do with Your Finished Resume

When you have your resume together, you've got to get it out. No one will notice you if you don't! Keep in mind the following suggestions when doing so.

Make sure your printed resume is always clean and neat.

> Put it in a folder or envelope so that it doesn't get wrinkled or dirty while you are checking out businesses for work.

Faxing is the most commonly requested form for submitting resumes.

> If you saved your resume on either a computer or disk and your computer has faxing software, you can just open your resume file in the word-processing program, choose the faxing software as the printer, and then complete the faxing process.

> If you saved your resume on either a computer or disk and your computer doesn't have faxing software, you can either print your resume or take a disk containing your file to your neighborhood copying or printing service and pay to have them print the resume and do the faxing. If you don't want to pay, you can always find someone who has a fax machine and ask if you can use it as well.

Emailing is becoming more popular as a means of sending and receiving resumes.

> If you saved your resume on either a computer or disk and your computer has Internet and emailing software, you can just attach the resume to an email message and send it off.

Mail a resume only when the company requires that method.

> If you mail your resume, make sure you address it in a professional manner and send it in a business envelope.

Each of these methods—faxing, emailing, or mailing a resume—requires that you send a cover letter too, so keep reading to find out how to create your own.

Writing Cover Letters

Picture this: José is looking for a job. He found out that the Computer Warehouse is hiring. José is really into computers so he thinks this position may be good for him. He goes to the store, asks for the manager, and, when the manager appears, begins talking. This is what José says:

> I have assisted various classmates in learning how to use basic computer software, successfully taken apart and put back together five computers, and I get along well with others. I am highly dedicated and motivated as well.

When José finishes talking, the manager just looks at him, as if to say, "Why are you telling me all this?"

What was José missing? He didn't give an introduction. Without defining who he was and stating what he wanted, José's conversation was meaningless to the employer. These are the functions of a cover letter in the job search process. To learn more, keep reading.

Cover Letters Allow You to Introduce Yourself

A cover letter is a brief, personalized letter that presents your resume. The overriding objective (or goal) for a cover letter is to let the employer know that you are interested in a specific position and to demonstrate your ability to perform the job. The cover letter sets the stage for the reader to accept your resume as something special; it's the first step to getting an interview and a job offer.

The standard length of a cover letter is three or four short paragraphs. The following list gives the purpose of each paragraph:

Paragraph 1: States the position you are applying for and where you heard about the opening

Paragraph 2-3: Highlights a few of your experiences that relate to the job that interests you

Final paragraph: Expresses your interest in the job and asks for a time to meet to talk more about what you could offer the company

---

Tips for Writing Cover Letters

- Always write with confidence and show a genuine interest in the job.
- Templated cover letters (cover letters that are pre-written to guide you through the writing process) are okay, but avoid sending a letter that reads as though you just filled in the blanks. Devise your own style so that you stand out from the crowd.
- Start powerfully; employers spend less than 30 seconds reading cover letters so the first sentence or two should pack a punch.

Here is an example of a cover letter:

123 4th Street
Somewhere, Washington 123456
(123) 234-5677

June 20, 2005

Coco Restaurant
123 5th Street
Somewhere, Washington 123456

Dear Mr. Suarez,

I am submitting my resume in response to the ad for full time servers at Coco Restaurant. I found the advertisement in the *Washington Reader* on Monday, June 19. Please review the enclosed resume to learn more about my qualifications.

I have varied experience in the restaurant and customer service fields, and I am looking for employment that will help develop my skills as I continue my education. As you will notice, I have experience in waiting tables, with the cash register, and in customer service. In addition, I am a motivated and dependable and will make an excellent addition to your staff.

After reviewing my resume, I am sure you will agree that my experiences make me an outstanding candidate for your position openings. If you have any additional questions or to set up an interview, please call me at (123) 234-5677. Thank you for reviewing my resume. I look forward to hearing from you soon.

Sincerely,

Andre Summers

Enclosure

Power Cover Letters

Cover letters need to pack a punch—that is, they need to catch the reader's attention immediately. To do this, use phrases that demonstrate your interest and enthusiasm for the job. Following are examples of "power" phrases to use when writing the different parts of a cover letter. Let's start with powerful introduction. Choose only one from these three examples.

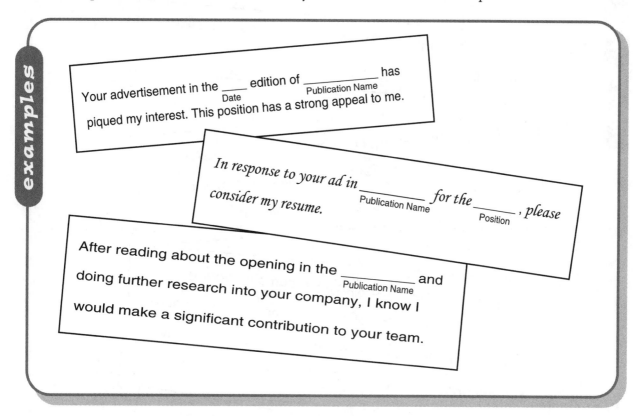

Your advertisement in the _____ edition of _____ has
Date   Publication Name
piqued my interest. This position has a strong appeal to me.

In response to your ad in _____ for the _____ , please
Publication Name   Position
consider my resume.

After reading about the opening in the _____ and
Publication Name
doing further research into your company, I know I
would make a significant contribution to your team.

Next are powerful sentences you can use in the body paragraphs, or main part, of your cover letter.

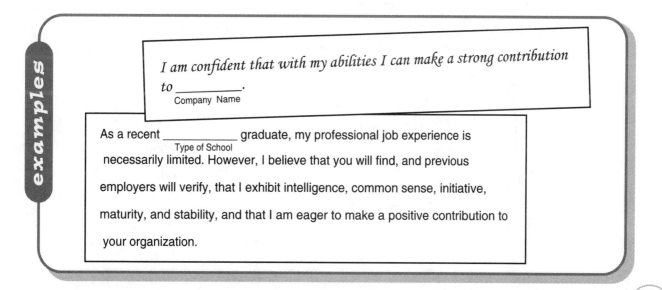

I am confident that with my abilities I can make a strong contribution
to _____.
Company Name

As a recent _____ graduate, my professional job experience is
Type of School
necessarily limited. However, I believe that you will find, and previous

employers will verify, that I exhibit intelligence, common sense, initiative,

maturity, and stability, and that I am eager to make a positive contribution to

your organization.

Your closing should state that you are definitely interested in the position and the company. Look at these powerful sentences for closing your cover letter.

examples

I would welcome the opportunity for a personal interview to further discuss my qualifications.

I wish to be part of an organization that wants to excel in ____ and ____. I believe that if I had the opportunity to interview with you, it would be apparent that my skills are far-reaching.
(Product, Product)

Please find enclosed a copy of my resume for your review. I believe the combination of my ____ and my ____ experience offers me the unique opportunity to make a positive contribution to your firm.
(Skill, Business)

I would appreciate an opportunity to discuss my abilities in more depth and am available for an interview at your earliest convenience.

With my training and hands-on experience, I know I can contribute to ____ and want to talk with you about it in person.
(Position)

You can use the preceding powerful phrases or make up some of your own in a cover letter that catches the attention and interest of any prospective employer. Remember, though, whenever you are writing something that others will read and question you about, make sure that you know what you are writing. Don't copy some big phrases that sound good just because they are in a book. If you don't frequently use a word or you don't know the definitions of words, *don't* use them. The employer will pick up right away that you did not put together your own resume or cover letter. Make sure to change the phrases to fit your style (but cut out the slang).

Practice Makes Perfect: Create Your Own Cover Letter

You're looking through the *Town Paper* when you come across the following job listing:

> #1 Company is looking for enthusiastic and dependable individuals for full-time sales position. Must have excellent communication skills, be outgoing, and work well with others. Fax or send your resume to: #1 Company Attn: Marco Maldanado, 123 ABC Street, Anytown, CA 12378 (333) 567-8900.

practice

You are interested in the position, and you have your resume ready. Now all you need is a cover letter to send with it. On your disk, create a cover letter that is sure to get you the job.

Your Cover Letter Checklist

Typing rather than handwriting any communication you are sending to a business is best—it looks more professional. If you don't have a computer at home, most schools and libraries have one that is accessible to you. Before printing and sending out your cover letter, make sure that it

- ❏ Addresses a person, not a title.
- ❏ Shows energy and enthusiasm for the job.
- ❏ Is brief and to the point.
- ❏ Includes information relevant to job you are seeking. (In other words, don't talk about some accomplishment that doesn't relate to the job just because you want to look good.)
- ❏ Avoids using the same phrases that the job description uses.
- ❏ Is direct. (Avoid sounding shy and timid; employers want out-going, confident workers.)
- ❏ Asks for an interview clearly and without apology or arrogance.

- ❏ Uses action verbs.
- ❏ Has varied sentence structures and short sentences (under 20 words).
- ❏ Is the standard length of one page of three or four short paragraphs.
- ❏ Has correct spelling and grammar.
- ❏ Has the correct spelling of the name of the company and the hiring person. (Check the spelling of this information more than once.)
- ❏ Has your signature at the bottom of the letter.
- ❏ Is proofread. (Have a couple of people who are good writers or editors do the proofreading.)

Creating Thank-You Notes

Finally. You've gone through the application process and just walked out of an interview. You were a bit nervous, but you made it, and it seemed as though things went well. The employer told you she would contact you within two weeks to let you know whether you were hired, so what do you do now? Don't just sit there waiting for the call, follow up with a thank-you note.

If you really want the job, you need to make a good impression, even after you walk out. Sending a thank-you note shows the employer that you are serious about your career and gives you an edge in the decision-making process. To make the best impression, make sure your thank-you note follows the guidelines given in the tips.

Tips for Writing Thank-You Notes

- Thank the employer for the interview.

- Express your interest in the position.

- Demonstrate the match between your skills and the job duties.

- Include your contact information.

- Make it brief (five to seven sentences max).

- Make sure that it fits on a small, blank thank-you note card.

- Mail it within 48 hours of your interview.

- Check it for correct spelling and grammar.

Misspellings and improper grammar may seem minor, but they send strong negative messages to an employer. The only thing worse than not sending a thank-you note is to send one with spelling errors.

Thank-You Notes Make a Good Impression

Following are some examples of ways to start your thank-you note. As with a cover letter, you want to be creative in how you write your note. Make the note short, but powerful. Remember: You need to demonstrate that you are the best person for the position.

examples

Thank you for meeting with me on _____. It was an enjoyable and
Date
informative interview. I came away very enthusiastic about the position you are seeking to fill.

I would like to take this opportunity to thank you for the interview this morning and to express my strong interest in the position of _____.

Thank you for the time you gave me to discuss the available position. The information you shared with me increased my desire to work for your company.

I would like to thank you for the interview on _____. I was very
Date
impressed with your company, and I am enthusiastic about the prospect of joining your team.

Practice Makes Perfect: Send Thank-You Notes

While writing a thank-you note for an interview you haven't really been to isn't easy, writing one for something else you appreciate is. To practice writing thank-you notes, think of something someone has done for you or even a past interview you went to (whether you interviewed for a job or something else). Write and send a thank-you note to that person. Use the following questions to help you.

practice makes perfect

Who should receive this thank-you note? _____

What did this person do for you? _____

_____

What did you gain from this person's time, support, and assistance? _____

_____

Use this space to write your note.

_____

_____

_____

_____

_____

_____

_____

_____

_____

_____

_____

_____

_____

_____

_____

_____

Role-Playing: Choose the Best Candidate

It's time to be the boss.

Your company, Computer Inc., is currently hiring. You placed the following ad and received four responses. You've conducted all the interviewing and are trying to make a decision. Read through the cover letters and thank-you notes from each candidate and make your decision.

COMPUTER INC. JOB POSTING

Web site Developer

We are currently seeking a Web site Developer to furnish professional Web site design and management advice. Web site Developer is responsible for performing a variety of administrative and technical work in planning and implementing the content of the firm's Web site, including the creation of unique content and design and integration of approved content from other sources. Candidate will work under the direction of the Information Technology Director and the Marketing Director.

Job Responsibilities:

Presents a consistent visual image through uniform fonts, formatting, icons, images, and layout techniques

Works with content authors ensuring adherence to applicable Web-language coding standards and currency of Web links; optimizes Web architecture for navigability ensuring the content quality and style of the site

Integrates new technology into the Web environment; maintains cross-platform and cross-browser compatibility; investigates new Web features and tools for use in authoring documents and managing the Web site.

Job Requirements:

2+ years of vocational, technical, or college training in computer science or graphic design

3+ years experience in Web site design and maintenance in a large organization, preferably a professional services organization

Experience with Web software, database design and implementation, and Web server to email interfaces

Considerable knowledge of graphics applications; working knowledge of standard Internet protocols; working knowledge of common Web languages; working knowledge of Internet and intranet connectivity protocols and software

Candidate must be skilled in Web site design and maintenance including server platforms and Web server software; database design and implementation

Ability to interact effectively with all levels of staff; ability to communicate effectively orally and in writing; and ability to demonstrate project management skills.

123 Main Street
Atlanta, Georgia 123456

(333) 234-5678

January 1, 2005

Computers Inc.
3456 Technology Drive Suite 246
New York, New York 12001

Dear Mr. Jones

Please accept the enclosed resume as application for the position Website Developer with Computer Inc. The position description matches my career interests and will utilize my educational background and previous employment experiences.

The position of Website Developer requires experience using knowledge and skills of which I have extensive experience in order to meet the individual needs of Computers Inc. As a recent graduate of Murray State University with a Bachelor of Science degree in Computer Science, I have had experience with not only determining the nature of data processing problems, but also website design. I am confident that my background in business and website engineering will allow me to devise or improve your current systems. During a cooperative education experience, I had the responsibility of designing various websites for several technology firms. I want to apply my skills to Computer Inc. as the company is highly regarded as being one of the top ten successful corporations in 1999, according to Computer Digest.

Please consider my request for a personal interview to discuss further employment opportunities. Please feel free to contact me at your earliest convenience at (333) 234-5678. I look forward to speaking with you soon. Thank you for your time and consideration.

Sincerely,

Marcy Raymonds

Enclosure: Resume

123 Main Street
Atlanta, Georgia 123456
(333) 234-5678

January 23, 2005

Computers Inc.
3456 Technology Drive Suite 246
New York, New York 12001

Dear Mr. Jones

Thank you for taking the time to discuss the Website Developer position at Computer Inc., with me. After meeting with you and observing the company's operations, I am further convinced that my background and skills coincide well with your needs.

I really appreciate that you took so much time to acquaint me with the company. It is no wonder that Computer Inc. retains its employees for so long. I feel I could learn a great deal from you and would certainly enjoy working with you.

In addition to my qualifications and experience, I will bring excellent work habits and judgment to this position. With the countless demands on your time, I am sure that you require people who can be trusted to carry out their responsibilities with minimal supervision.

I look forward, Mr. Jones, to hearing from you concerning your hiring decision. Again, thank you for your time and consideration.

Sincerely,

Marcy Raymonds

367 Any Street
Shaker Heights, Ohio 34555
(444) 546-6789

January 1, 2005

Computers Inc.
3456 Technology Drive Suite 246
New York, New York 12001

Dear Sir or Madame:

I am interested in job opportunities as a Websit Developer. I have complete responsibility for freelance projects for a variety of companies where I created websites and used a wide range of styles to offer multiple ideas and variations to fulfill client needs. My experience involves using a wide assortment of hardware and software, and I continu to expand my capabilities with any technology that will help me to achieve new and exciting results. Having proven my organizational skills, and managed time and resources, I am currently interested in a position that would utilize my spills and offer me additional responsibilities and new challenges. I am a team player but also work well on individual assignments. If you are looking for a capable, professional, high-energy individuale to fill a position in your company, please give me a call. Thank you for your time.

Sincerely,

Joe Josephs

Enclosure: Resume

367 Any Street
Shaker Heights, Ohio 34555
(444) 546-6789

January 23, 2005

Computers Inc.
3456 Technology Drive Suite 246
New York, New York 12001

Dear Mr. Jones,

Thank you so much for taking the time to interview me today for the website developer position.

I felt a wonderful rapport not only with you, but with the whole Computer Inc. staff. I am more convinced than ever that I will fit in as a member of the team and contribute my skills and talents for the benefit of your company.

I can make myself available for any further discussions of my qualifications that may be needed.

Again, Mr. Jones, I very much appreciate you and your staff taking so much time to talk with me about this exciting opportunity.

Sincerely,

Joe Josephs

7784 Aire Street
Phoenix, Arizona 85467
(777) 862-3456

January 1, 2005

Computers Inc.
3456 Technology Drive Suite 246
New York, New York 12001

Dear Mr. Jones,

The attached resume is submitted for your evaluation with regards to all available positions applicable to my credentials. I am employed at present with Expansion Computers, but I wish to find employment that affords me greater challenges, rewards and compensation than the organization can provide for me.

I have a record of outstanding success in the creation of innovative solutions concerning web design and programming, including visual basic, website design, multimedia and systems-based problem solving for both Windows and Macintosh based applications. My expertise utilizes both personal creativity and technical knowledge, and I have extensive experience in: graphic design, screen-printing, computer-based graphic design, spreadsheet and database creation, illustration, computer programming and photography, in addition to my web-design experience. My leadership skills were considerably enhanced by an appointment as an interim art director right after I had graduated high school. I have 10 years experience in computer operations and computer programming, and 17 years in web and graphic design and illustration covering.

My four years of working for Expansion Computers has encompassed a wide-range of responsibilities, from trouble-shooting and correcting problems on all types of Windows and DOS-based computer systems to designing departmental publications for distribution state-wide, writing installation programs for financial budgetary software and designing and maintaining websites.

My resume provides a good summary of my background and general experience. Please contact me as soon as possible, as I would like to arrange a mutually convenient time for a meeting, during which we can further discuss your current or anticipated openings.

Sincerely,

Jose Sanchez

Enclosure: Resume

7784 Aire Street
Phoenix, Arizona 85467
(777) 862-3456

January 23, 2005

Computers Inc.
3456 Technology Drive Suite 246
New York, New York 12001

Dear Mr. Jones,

I would like to thank you for talking with me about the website developer position at Computer Inc. I truly appreciate all the time and care you took in telling me about the job and learning more about me.

I am so pleased that you agree that my extensive work in the technology field provides me with excellent experience for this position. I am eager to bring my passion for this line of work to the website developer position, and I am convinced the knowledge and experience I've already cultivated make me the best researcher for the job.

I very much look forward to learning of your decision soon. Please feel free to contact me if you need more information about my qualifications. Thank you again for the interview.

Sincerely,

Jose Sanchez

5649 Mango Street
Chicago, Illinois 60001
(889) 489-3334

January 1, 2003

Computers Inc.
3456 Technology Drive Suite 246
New York, New York 12001

Dear Mr. Jones,

Currently, I am a Network Systems Engineer with an excellent record of accomplishment and success in my field. Highlights of my background include Microsoft MCSE on NT4 & 2000, Cisco CCNA & CCDA, and Master Certified Internet Webmaster Administrator certifications. I believe that my qualifications, along with my drive and determination, would make me an excellent candidate for a position with any company.

I have worked with Visual Basic (COM, ActiveX), SQL Server (Stored Procedures), FrontPage, Web, HTML, DreamWeaver, and C++. I have experienced in building VB and Access database from the beginning to the end and designed Intersection Signals for Department of Transportation.

My success in the past has stemmed from my strong commitment and sense of professionalism. I keep high standards for my work and am known for my ability to follow through.

I would like to be considered as a serious candidate for the position of website developer and look forward to pursuing this avenue with you further. Thank you for your time and attention.

Sincerely,

Marc Jackson

Enclosure: Resume

Marc Jackson did not send a thank-you note to Mr. Jones.

You have just read a sample job posting for a Web site Developer position and four different cover letters and thank-you notes submitted for the position. Answer the following questions to determine who would make the best candidate.

Write your answers in the blanks.

1. Based on the cover letters and thank you-notes, which candidate made the best impression for the position? Rank the candidates from 1-4, 1 being the most favorable impression and 4 being the least favorable impression.

    Marcy Raymonds   _____

    Joe Josephs   _____

    Jose Sanchez   _____

    Marc Jackson   _____

2. What makes your number 1 candidate stand out? _____

    _____

3. What makes your number 4 candidate the least desirable? _____

    _____

4. Are there aspects of your candidates 2 and 3 that could have made them number 1? What are they? _____

    _____

5. What are some things that the your number 4 candidate could have done differently to improve his/her standing? _____

    _____

    _____

---

holla' zone: *a place for you to let out your thoughts*

cover letters and thank-you notes are not just for job interviews. remember: their purposes are to introduce you, what you are looking for, and then to thank employers for giving their time to you. you can use the same concept for applying to schools, for scholarships, to get into special programs, as well as a variety of other purposes. some people feel that it's not necessary to use these techniques, and yet they still get a job, into that school or program, or that scholarship.

for this holla' zone, reflect on the purpose of these two communications pieces and think about the following questions:

why would it be beneficial for you to use a cover letter (or some form of introduction of yourself) and follow up with a thank-you note to people?

are these tools useful only for the person reading them, or are there some personal benefits to writing them?

if so, what are the personal benefits of these pieces?

write your responses to these questions in a paragraph.

_____

_____

_____

_____

_____

keepin' it real

Karina and Sean both interviewed for a job at Buyers Market. Both were qualified for the job and left a good impression with the manager, so when it came down to making the hiring decision, the manager was really struggling.

While taking a break from the decision-making process, the manager checked the mail for that day. In it, he found a short thank-you note from Sean. It was a very simple letter, thanking the manager for taking the time to interview Sean and commenting that Sean was really impressed with the company and would enjoy working there. After reading the letter, the manager made his decision, and Sean started working the next week.

meta - Instant Message

see, putting together your resume isn't as hard as you thought, is it? and the benefits of it, as well as the cover letter and thank-you notes, definitely outweigh the work that went in. just remember when you go out to find your next job, these tools will impact your search greatly. let them speak for you so that when you get to the interview, it will be smooth sailing.

Ready for Tryouts?

Prepping for an Interview

In this chapter, you will:

- Tell your two-minute story
- Practice interviewing

Get to the point:

These final steps are crucial in landing a job, so if you don't know how to interview, just read on!

Think of an interview as your personal commercial. That's right. You can think of yourself as a product, and you want a company to buy you. As with any product, you have to go into an interview knowing that you are the best product out there and that company would be missing out if they didn't hire you. In order to do that, you have to approach an interview with confidence and know what you want, which requires you to have spent some time thinking about what you want out of life and your job. Whoa! That's kind of intimidating, isn't it?

Are you asking yourself if it's worth it? Think about it. Some of your friends have jobs; your family members have jobs; and many other people do, too. Many of them probably didn't spend a lot of time trying to figure out what they wanted. They may have just looked in the

newspaper for a job that was open in a field that they liked and took the first job offer they received. So why can't you do that? You can, but if you want to get a really good job and be successful, you have to take this time to really consider what it is you want to do with your life. Aren't a few hours of prep work before an interview worth a few extra (or even a few thousand) dollars and a job you enjoy?

What you need to realize is that while you are thinking, "I really need a job, please let them hire me," the people in a company are often thinking, "We really need a quality employee. Could this be that person?" It's as though they are saying, "*Please* let this be the right person. We're tired of interviewing, and we really need someone." More often than not, if you can present yourself in a manner that shows you will be an asset to the company, the employer will be more than happy to hire you and adjust a bit to your needs. The interview, then, is the place where both sides—the interviewer and interviewee—come to find out about each other and how they can meet each other's needs.

Thus, it is very important that you prepare yourself for an interview (especially if you want to be happy with where you work). It is important to understand that an interview is not only your self-marketing technique, but also a way for you to learn more about the company to see whether you want to work there. Yes, this process can be intimidating, especially if this is your first interview, but don't worry. By the end of this chapter, you will be a pro and go through your first (or next) interview with flying colors.

---

meta - Instant Message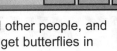

even after interviewing more than 20 times in my life, having interviewed other people, and teaching people how to interview, i still get nervous. not overly, but I still get butterflies in my stomach sometimes. to calm myself, i pray, go over all my assets, and think to myself that no matter what the outcome, it's all going to work out. if it's where i'm supposed to be, even if i mess up a little, i'll still get the job.

the worst interview I ever had was probably the second interview for my position working with homeless youth. the executive director told me over the phone that i would be doing part of my interview in spanish and also meeting one of the founders of the organization. i was a bit nervous because i hadn't been using my spanish very much at that time and didn't want to lose the job because of that. i was hoping to get the spanish part of the interview out of the way in the beginning, but that is not how it worked out. i met with the founder first and was so nervous because i kept thinking about the spanish part. i was trying to stay focused, but he is one of those interviewers who you can't read…you know, those kind who don't make any facial gestures as to whether they are impressed by what you say…i hate those types of interviews. anyway, i kept feeling like he wasn't impressed with my answers, plus i was already very nervous, so i felt so stumbly throughout the interview. i finally stopped the interview and apologized. i told him i was very nervous for the spanish part of the interview. i explained that although i knew spanish, i still got nervous when i was tested, and i didn't want to mess up. that helped to break the ice, and he told me not to worry. the rest of our interview went well, and when it came to the spanish, i did fine. fortunately, i got the position and really enjoyed my job.

Go in Prepped: Know What They'll Ask

The interviewing is the crucial part of your job search. If you've made it this far, you want to do all you can to make a good impression, as it could mean the end of your search, at least for now. To be successful, you have to be prepared, but how can you do that when you don't know what questions they will ask. In this section, you will cover some common questions in an interview and discover creative ways for handling almost any question that is thrown at you.

Tell Me About Yourself

Imagine that you've gone to the interview, sat down in front of the interviewer, said, "Hello," and the interviewer says to you, "So, tell me a little about yourself." What do you say?

This request is one of the most common during an interview, but if you haven't prepared for your interview, you'll sit there, eyes wide and mouth open, as if to say, "What do you want me to tell you?" This is not a good position to be in at an interview, especially if you really want this job. Let's work on how to answer this, which is really just your commercial about yourself.

One way to prepare your "self-marketing piece" for an interview is to prepare a two-minute story—a brief statement about yourself that shows your strengths, interests, and experiences. Each person's two-minute story is different. There is no exact formula for what to say. What is most important is that you express some positive facts about yourself and a brief background of your accomplishments so that the employer has an understanding of the real you—not just the side they would see at work. Here are some basic guidelines for what to include (and what *not* to include) in your "two-minute story." Read over the guidelines and then complete the activities following it.

Good	Not So Good
Current school/work status	Every detail of your life
(Expected) graduation date	Where you went to grammar school
Degrees/certificates obtained	Negative things about yourself
Experiences with other cultures	How many brothers and sisters you have
Activities involved in school, church, or community	Negative things about working or school
Best/favorite subjects	Talking (bad) about other people
Previous work experience	Gossip
Future goals	How desperately you need money or want the job
Interests	Favorite food/TV show/color/and so on

As mentioned, these are only suggestions. Keep in mind that some of the items in the "not-so-good" column are okay to use if they show how you may have overcome a difficult situation. For example, it's okay to mention that you grew up in a family with seven kids and you moved every year of your life until you were 12 *if* you briefly mention how that experience affected you in a positive way, such as: "Life was very difficult for me when I was growing up because I had a lot of responsibilities, and I never felt stable. It taught me, though, the value of family and to get along with new and different people."

Remember: The most important goal in writing a two-minute story is that you want to reflect positively on yourself and show the employer qualities you have that would benefit the company. Use your two-minute story to set yourself apart from other people!

Use your two-minute story to set yourself apart from other people!

You use a two-minute story during a job interview to give the employer a brief summary of your background, education, work experience, and explanation of your future interests and goals in less than two minutes. In order to formulate your own two-minute story, read over the suggestions in the following sections and complete the activity. If you actually have an interview coming up, answer the questions according to that particular job. If not, answer about a job you would be interested in having.

Think About the Future

Know yourself and what you want. Even if you aren't 100 percent sure, have an idea of your goals and interests, and your values, strengths, and weaknesses.

Think about and then answer the following questions, writing notes in the space provided:

1. What are your future career goals? (If you are not 100% sure, what are some fields that interest you?) _____

   _____

   _____

2. How would this type of job help you reach your future goals? _____

   _____

   _____

Remember Your Past

Reflect on past experiences before going into interview. List all the jobs, volunteer experiences, classes that relate to your career interest, awards and honors, and extra activities you have been involved in. Tell how long you were involved, your duties, accomplishments, specific skills required for activity, and special recognition you have received.

Write the following information (you may want to go over your resume to help you remember some information):

Jobs	Length of Employment	Major Duties
_____	_____	_____
_____	_____	_____
_____	_____	_____

Volunteer Experiences	Length of Time	Major Duties
_____	_____	_____
_____	_____	_____
_____	_____	_____

Classes	When Did You Take It	Skills Developed
_____	_____	_____
_____	_____	_____
_____	_____	_____

Extracurricular Activities	Length of Time	Skills Developed
_____	_____	_____
_____	_____	_____
_____	_____	_____

Awards and Recognitions	When Received
_____	_____
_____	_____
_____	_____

Be Passionate

An interview is the best time to give an employer the sense that you have passion for the job. Even if you're interviewing for your first job and you don't know that it is exactly what you want to do for the rest of your life, it is good to show an eagerness to work and learn more about what the company does. If you can show your sincerity, genuine interest, and dedication, you're more than likely to get the job. Find the qualities inside of you that make you a good worker and have examples from your life experiences that back them up such as the one Flora used:

> Flora has an interview at a day care center. When asked why she applied for the position, she responded, "I love children. I have four nieces and nephews, and my neighborhood is filled with children. I constantly offer to watch them, so a day doesn't go by that I am not with a child. Usually the kids have so much fun playing games and doing activities with me that they don't even want to leave."

What would you say to an employer about why you want to do the job? Write your answer in the following space.

_____

_____

_____

_____

_____

Become One with the Company

To be successful in an interview, not only should you convey a desire for the job, but you must also be able to explain why you'd be a good fit for the job. Demonstrating your ability to handle that position requires that you know what the job involves and have some background about the company. The more you can demonstrate your ability to function effectively in that position, the better chance you have of being hired. Remember: Companies are not looking for someone who is perfect, just someone who will work hard and is willing to grow and learn.

What are characteristics you have that would make you a good employee for any company?

_____

_____

_____

_____

_____

Practice Makes Perfect: Create Your Own Two-Minute Story

Now you can't just think about your answer to the questions in the previous worksheet and just come up with a two-minute story. You've actually got to spend some time working out exactly what you are going to say. I'm not suggesting you go into an interview with a memorized speech or notes written on the back of your hand. That just wouldn't be right. But having a better handle on what you're going to say helps to calm down any nervousness that you may feel. So, take this time to actually write out your two-minute story. Remember: What you say when you are in the interview may not come out exactly as you have written it, but whatever you say will come across as a though you are a person who has really taken some time to examine your life.

practice makes perfect

My Two-Minute Story

_____
_____
_____
_____
_____
_____
_____
_____
_____
_____
_____

holla' zone: a place for you to let out your thoughts

no one else in the world is quite like you, so why would you want to interview like anyone else? you are not made up of just your work and educational achievements. many of these experiences are guided by your personal experiences. if you really want to stand apart from other potential employees, you need to personalize your interview. think of an experience in your life that has led you to do what it is that you want to do, either right now or in your future. write notes about that event and how and why it has influenced your life.

_____
_____
_____
_____
_____
_____
_____
_____
_____

What Are Your Weaknesses?

Employers often ask you about your weaknesses and failures. These questions can be tricky because you don't want to come across as a poor employee, but you know employers are not looking for you to say that you have none. So how do you answer these? Keep reading for some hints on how to answer to these questions.

Turn Negatives into Positives

You're not perfect, huh? You may not always get along with people, you may have failed once, twice, or even 20 times, or you may not be the smartest kid on the block, but you can still get a job *if* you leave all the drama outside the interview door. This doesn't mean that you can't talk about your failures or weaknesses, because you will probably be asked about them, but rather it means finding a way to talk about some of the not-so-good features of your life (because none of us are perfect) in a positive manner. The following sections give you some tips for doing that.

Use Each Question as a Way to Talk About Your Strengths

Knowing that no one is perfect, an employer will most likely ask about your weaknesses or a time when you have failed. It is okay to talk about these things, but show how you overcame these obstacles and are working to improve yourself in these areas. Your willingness to grow and learn both personally and professionally is an asset most companies want.

When you talk about your weaknesses, remember that you never want to say something that makes you look bad, such as "I'm always late." That type of statement is sure to lose you any chance of getting that job. While lateness may be a weakness for you, find something else to say. Always follow up your weakness with an example of how you are working to be better in this are. For example, if you get bored easily, you may say, "I have a tendency to get bored during school, so I found ways to make topics more realistic so that I can apply them to my life."

A common question in an interview is "What is your greatest weakness?" How would you answer this to make a weakness sound like a strong point?

_____

_____

_____

_____

_____

Show Perseverance Through Tough Situations

At times, things on the job go wrong and, if it is not fixed, the company or you could end up looking bad. Employers want to know inventive ways you've dealt with problems that no one foresaw. When preparing for the interview, think of examples that demonstrate your willingness, ability, and eagerness to go the extra mile to get the job done right.

Write about a time when it looked as though you were going to fail, but you put in some extra effort and everything worked out.

_____
_____
_____
_____
_____

Emphasize Educational Achievements If You Lack Job Experience

If you have never had a job because you are still in high school, state that. Discuss the positive contributions you have made in school, home, and through your activities. Try to provide examples of how you can use the skills required at school on the job. Also include comments such as, "I am willing to learn and want to know more about what types of work suit me so I can make informed decisions about my future."

List some of the skills you have and then write how you can use them on the job.

Skill	Use on the Job
_____	_____
_____	_____
_____	_____
_____	_____

Be Respectful of Others

Never criticize a former employer, or anyone else for that matter, during an interview. It may be that the person you are putting down is someone they know and respect. Additionally, you gain respect if you can acknowledge any tensions or problems, but still talk respectfully about that person. For example, if an employer asks about your school performance, and a former teacher and you didn't get along well, which affected your performance in school, you could say, "The teacher's style of teaching was hard for me to comprehend. I did not feel that the teacher understood me, so unfortunately I chose not to participate in the class." That's better than saying, "That teacher didn't know how to teach and was so boring. I couldn't stand him, so I stopped doing my work."

Is there a time when you didn't get along with a teacher or supervisor? What happened? What are some positive things you can say about that person? What are some things you learned from that experience? Write a paragraph, describing your experience.

_____

_____

_____

_____

_____

_____

Don't Hide

Many people fear job interviews because of age, their past, or lack of experience, so they often approach the job search with a "Please-I-am-begging-you-please-please-please-give-me-a-job. I'll-do-anything-I-promise" attitude when it comes to trying to get a job. This comes across in their voice, in the way they hold themselves, and in the way they answer questions.

True enough, you can't change your age, past, or how much experience you (don't) have, but those factors don't mean that you can't learn new skills and do a job effectively. Don't hide behind your past and think that you can't do better for yourself because you can. You need to go into a job situation with confidence and try to show an employer that, yes, you may be young, have some blemishes on your record, or lack experience, but you are determined to learn, grow, and change, and you are willing to take on the challenges that this job presents.

What are some things you are willing to do to show that you are prepared to move past your past?

_____

_____

_____

_____

_____

_____

_____

holla' zone: *a place for you to let out your thoughts*

no one likes to admit failures, but the reality is that everyone has them. while many people try to hold you back by reminding you of your failures, you don't have to let that happen. recalling your failures can help show you where you messed up so that you can learn from those mistakes. for this holla' zone, think of one of your failures and write it down. then write what you have learned from that experience and how you can use that to improve yourself.

_____

_____

_____

_____

_____

What Are the Other Common Interview Questions?

Some people prepare for an interview by reviewing commonly asked question and then create and memorize responses to those questions. This can be helpful, but what if you aren't asked any of those questions? To better prepare yourself, do not memorize answers. Instead, think of some challenges in your work and life background–positive and negative–and think of answers to those challenges, your response, and the results. You can use these examples throughout the interview by tailoring them to the questions the interviewer asks.

Employers have definite concerns when deciding to hire someone. If you can demonstrate the following characteristics, you will improve your chances at getting the job.

- **Suitability:** Do you have the necessary skills, and does it appear that you will be a good fit for this organization?
- **Determination:** Are you going to tough it out if things get rough?
- **Flexibility:** How do you respond to constructive criticism if you make a mistake? Do you run or grow?
- **Problem-solving attitude:** If a problem arises, do you try to come up with solutions or do you just let it go and let someone else deal with the problem?
- **Team player:** Do you work well with others?

While Chapter 4 discusses these characteristics, keep in mind that these are questions that the employer is trying to answer in his or her head as you are interviewing. You need to prepare your responses to demonstrate these traits. Think about these traits when you are going through the following activity.

Practice Makes Perfect: Answer the Interview Questions

Give the following list of questions to a friend or someone you know. Have that person randomly select four questions (one from each category) and use the questions to interview you. To better prepare for your interview, you should not know which questions the interviewer will ask you. If you actually have an interview scheduled, have the person pretend you are interviewing for that specific job. If you don't have a specific job in mind, think of a job you would like to have and have the person interview you as though you were applying for that job.

Using the following list of questions, have someone ask you four questions from each section. For each question asked, record the following information:

- Write your response to the question.
- Indicate how comfortable you felt answering the question: Circle V for **V**ery comfortable, S for **S**omewhat comfortable, and **N** for Not comfortable.
- Write reminders for yourself on how you can improve.

General Questions	Response	Comfort Level (Circle one)	Suggestions for Improvement
What can I do for you today?		V S N	
What is the position you are applying for?		V S N	
How did you learn of this position?		V S N	
What kind of work interests you most?		V S N	
What qualities are necessary to succeed in this type of work?		V S N	
What about this position interests you?		V S N	
What can you do for the company?		V S N	
Education Questions			
How much education do you have?		V S N	
Do you plan to go to college?		V S N	
What do you intend to study?		V S N	
What are your favorite subjects?		V S N	
What activities are you involved in at school?		V S N	
Give me an example of a time you demonstrated leadership.		V S N	

practice makes perfect

Education Questions	Response	Comfort Level (Circle one)	Suggestions for Improvement
What is your least favorite subject?		V S N	
Your grade point average is low. Can you explain why that is?		V S N	
Work-Related Questions			
How will you get to work?		V S N	
Do you have a driver's license?		V S N	
What sort of work schedule are you looking for?		V S N	
How many hours a week can you work?		V S N	
Do you have any personal situation that would prevent you from getting to work on time?		V S N	
What shift do you want to work?		V S N	
Can you work weekends?		V S N	
Have you worked in the past?		V S N	
What sort of experience do you have?		V S N	
If you have never worked, what sort of skills do you have that would benefit the company?		V S N	
What did you like most about your last job?		V S N	
What did you like least about your last job?		V S N	
What do you know about this job?		V S N	
What do you know about our company?		V S N	
Why do you want to work for this company?		V S N	
Give me an example of how well you work with others.		V S N	

(continues)

(continued)

Work-Related Questions	Response	Comfort Level (Circle one)	Suggestions for Improvement
How well do you take instruction?		V S N	
What sort of management style suits you?		V S N	
What are your expectations of a supervisor?		V S N	
What do you do if you have a disagreement with another employee?		V S N	
What would you do if you became bored with work?		V S N	
Why do you think you would be successful in this position?		V S N	
Do you work well under pressure?		V S N	
You and Your Future Questions			
Describe your personality.		**V S N**	
What is your major weakness?		**V S N**	
What do you like to do in your spare time?		**V S N**	
What is your most important accomplishment?		**V S N**	
What are your plans for the future?		**V S N**	
How does this position relate to your career goals?		**V S N**	
What is your philosophy on life?		**V S N**	
Describe yourself in three words.		**V S N**	

Antonio had applied for a position as a supervisor, something he had never done before, but was confident that he could handle the position. Because he was only 23, he knew his age might be a barrier to getting the position. Fortunately, Antonio had very clear goals for his life, was highly motivated, and made the most of the opportunities presented to him. While interviewing, Antonio pointed out that, although he was young, he had been through many life experiences that qualified him for the position and showed his dedication. He discussed his goals, and, throughout the interview, it was obvious that he had a passion for the job for which he was interviewing. At the end of the interview, the supervisor was so impressed that she hired him on the spot. Later, Antonio learned that everyone else who was hired in that department had had to go through a second interview process before the company made a final decision.

What They Don't Need to Know: Questions You Don't Have to Answer

Employers want to know as much information as possible about a potential candidate so that they can feel comfortable that they are making the right decision. Let's face it: If you own a business, you don't want to waste a lot of time, money, and other resources on an employee who's going to be around for just a few weeks. You want someone who will help your company grow. The more the employers know about the candidate, the easier it is for them to make a decision.

However, employers *don't* need to ask you some things. In fact, federal laws prohibit employers from asking certain questions. Before going into an interview, you should know what you *don't* have to answer so that you can protect yourself. The following topics are *not* supposed to be questions during an interview:

- Race
- Gender
- Religion
- Marital status
- Age
- Physical and/or mental status
- Ethnic background
- Country of origin
- Sexual preference
- Any other discriminatory factors that are illegal for making employment decisions

Unless a specific job function requires this information, an employer shouldn't ask questions about these topics. If the interview appears to be moving in that direction, however, your best bet is to try to keep it focused on the requirements of the position and your qualifications as a candidate. Blatant discrimination does take place. If it does and you are offended, you have the right to end the interview immediately.

If you are asked questions about one of these topics, here are some actions you should or should not take.

- Don't act defensive in response to illegal questions. Many interviewers are just as inexperienced or as uncomfortable in interviewing as you are, and are looking for ways to ease into the interview.

- Answer truthfully if you feel your response will not hurt you.

- Inform the interviewer that the question is illegal. You may risk offending them and ending your chances for the position, but your integrity may often impress them and make you look more favorable for the position.

- If you choose to answer the question, base your answer on the requirements of the job and your ability to perform it.

Remember: Don't make a big scene if someone asks you illegal questions. Just be professional and bring it to their attention. If the person continues to pressure you for answers or you feel as though you are being discriminated against, don't hesitate to walk out. Most likely you won't get the job, but it's a job you probably don't want anyway. And remember, you can always take legal action if the person is way out of line.

holla' zone: *a place for you to let out your thoughts*

no matter how much or little experience you have, interviewing can be an intimidating process. knowing who you are and what you want makes that process easier. in order to get rid of pre-interview jitters, write down all those thoughts you have that make you nervous. after you have written all your thoughts, review your list and write at least one positive thought for each.

example:

nervous thought	positive thought
what if i don't have all the skills i need?	i may not have the skills, but i'm a quick learner, and i'm willing to give it a try.

Because you are not going to know exactly what questions an interviewer will ask, following these hints can help you prepare for almost any question thrown at you. Granted, sometimes employers ask trick questions to throw you off, but keep your cool during these questions and you'll do just fine. Also, keep in mind that often the most qualified person is not the one who lands the job; it's the one who interviews the best. To be the most effective interviewee, follow the suggestions in this section.

You Get to Ask Questions Too!

Many young people go to a first interview thinking, "I really need a job, and I hope the employer will hire me." They're so focused on just getting a job that they forget to stop and think about why they want a job and what the job for can do for their future. When they go into an interview, they are totally unprepared.

The purpose of an interview is not just so that an employer can find out about you. What an interview is supposed to be is a conversation between you and the employer so that you can find out more about each other to see if you are a good match. It's sort of like a dating game: The interviewer finds out about you, and you find out about the company.

Think about it. You wouldn't want to spend your life with someone you couldn't get along with after two hours, so why would you want to work at a place you couldn't stand after a few hours? After you are out of school, your place of employment becomes the place where you spend much of your daily life, so you might as well find a job you enjoy. And, to be quite honest, if you go into an interview without questions for the employer, your interview won't stand out.

If you can demonstrate that you have checked out the company and are looking out for what's best for the company and you, you become a more attractive candidate. And it helps you to know whether you'll be able to do and learn the things you want to learn in that job. This section will help guide you through your interviewing process.

Why Should I Accept This Job?

Because an important part of interviewing is the interviewee asking questions about the company and position, you need to prepare some questions to ask an employer during the interview. To start, look in the classified section of a newspaper or on the Internet for a job that interests you. It doesn't have to be a job that you could work now, just a job that you find interesting. Following are some thought joggers that can help you formulate questions about a company or career.

Personal Information
- Job responsibilities
- Describe a typical day
- Good and bad points about the job
- Challenges in job
- The skills or personal qualities needed
- The potential for growth within the company
- The potential for personal development on the job

Business Related
- The products or services offered
- Length of time in business
- Work atmosphere
- Company mission
- Leading competitors–who are they and how do the companies compare

General Questions About the Field
- What are the challenges in the field today?
- What is the future of the field?
- How has the field changed in last ten years?
- Are any professional organizations associated with the field?
- How does an employee stay on top of new information for the field?
- What type of educational background do you need?
- Do you need any licenses?

Write ten questions that could help you decide whether a company or type of job is one you would like.

1. _____
2. _____
3. _____
4. _____
5. _____
6. _____
7. _____
8. _____
9. _____
10. _____

Practice Makes Perfect: Interview the Company

It's time to practice. For this project, you need to call the company you chose in the previous activity and arrange an interview with someone in the advertised position. You will use the questions you created in the previous activity to learn more about that position and company.

Keep in mind that the phone number from the ad may not lead to the person who has the information you need. Explain to the person who answers the phone that you are working on a project and are interested in finding out more about a particular position. Ask if he or she can direct you to the appropriate person (and remember to say "Thanks!"). If you don't feel comfortable calling a company or person you don't know, use some networking skills to find someone that you know (or a close friend or family member knows) in that field, and interview that person.

You can choose to do the interview either in person or over the phone. However, the person you want to interview may not have the time available right away to do the interview, so you need to give them some flexibility. If you want to do an interview over the phone, ask if they have time. If they can't at the moment, ask to please set a time that you could call and do the interview. Make sure you get an exact day and time. Don't say, "I'll just call back," or you'll never get an interview. If arranging the interview becomes very difficult, you may want to find someone else to interview.

Use the following scripts when scheduling interviews. Remember: Practice what you are going to say before calling so you don't sound as though you are reading, even if you are. Use Script 1 if someone refers you to a company. If you are calling a company you read about in the classified ads, use Script 2. (When you are connected to the correct person, use some of the text from Script 1 as a guide to what you should say.)

practice makes perfect

SCRIPT 1

Hello, my name is _____ , and I'm a student at _____ school. I was given your name by _____ who said you may be available to allow me to interview you. Currently, I am exploring career options, hoping to learn more about the industry. I would love the opportunity to get your thoughts and advice on the_____ field. It shouldn't take more than half an hour. When would it be convenient for you to meet or have a conversation? ..... Thank you.

SCRIPT 2

Hello, my name is _____ , and I'm a student at _____ school. I am calling hoping to speak to someone in the _____ department. I have a project for school in which I have to interview someone in a job that interests me. I found an ad for your company while going through the want ads, and I was hoping someone in the _____ department would be able to meet or talk with me over the phone to answer some questions I have prepared. It shouldn't take more than half an hour, and I need to have the project done by _____. Could you direct me to the appropriate person to speak with please?.... Thank you.

Use this space to write the responses you get from the person you interviewed.

_____
_____
_____
_____
_____
_____
_____
_____
_____
_____
_____
_____
_____
_____
_____
_____
_____
_____
_____
_____

holla' zone: *a place for you to let out your thoughts*

whew! you got it done. you actually interviewed the person about the job, and it wasn't as bad as you thought it would be. so now what? you're probably thinking, "how will this information help me in the future?" well, if you leave the interview as just that, an interview, it's not going to help you much, but if you actually take time to think about the information given and use it to help guide you for your own career search, you can gain important clues on some of the steps you need to take to become successful. so, use this section to reflect on your interview. think about some of the following questions:

- your impressions of the job
- how the job matches (or doesn't match) your interests
- how the interview impacted your career direction
- information about the company, including:

  products and services

  mission and goals

  work atmosphere
- who you interviewed and your impressions about that person

write a one-page paper about what you gained from the interview. write your notes here.

_____

_____

_____

_____

_____

_____

It's Your Turn to Shine: Acing the Interview

You're almost there. You have your interview scheduled, you've practiced, and you know how to get to the interview, but wait. There are a few more details that you can't forget. Sometimes it is the little things, like what you wear and your timing, that make or break the deal, and this is one deal you sure don't want to lose out on. Review the following sections so that you are equipped with all the inside scoop for getting this job.

Dress the Part

So, you've practiced what you are going to say at the interview, and you have all the information you need to bring. Now it's time to get ready, but what are you going to wear? Yeah, you've seen all those videos on how to dress for success, but, come on, you're young. Like you really want to wear a suit jacket… You need to look tight, right? Well, sort of. No, you don't have to give up your style, but you do have to remember that you are looking for a job. You will have to make some sacrifices. Sure, you look fine in those Pelle Pelle jeans and sweater, but your potential new boss may not be so cool wit' em, ya know. So, work with it. Find out how you can still keep your style while impressing the boss during your interview.

So, what do you wear to an interview? I know you have probably read all the formal lists of do's and don'ts. You know the following:

Men

Yes	No
Suit jacket	T-shirts
Button down shirt	Tank tops
Tie	Earrings
Khaki or dress pants	Jeans or shorts
Brown or black dress shoes	Gym shoes

Women

Yes	No
Dress	Mini skirts
Pant suit	See-through shirts
Skirt at least knee length	Tight clothing
Nylons	Gym shoes
Dress shoes, low heels	Open toe shoes
Light makeup	Bright or unusual colors (such as purple lipstick)

But, "Come on," you're thinking, "Remember, I'm young. I'm not comfortable in that. It doesn't look right on me." You may not have any clothes like those in the Yes list, and you (and your family) really do not have the money to go out and buy you the clothes right now. So, how can you make what is in your closet fit for an interview?

First, do as much as you can to follow the guidelines. Whatever doesn't work, read below for some more help.

Ladies

- Most importantly, be as conservative as possible.
- Avoid tops that have words on the front, come off the shoulder, or have splits in the fabric.

- Avoid jean dresses or skirts.
- Instead of a suit jacket, wear a solid color button-down sweater. You don't have to button it.
- Don't wear tight fitting clothes, period.
- Capri pants and shorts are not acceptable. If you wear pants, stick to dress slacks that are not tight fitting.
- No hats.
- Try to avoid fragrances, but, if you choose to wear some, keep it light.
- Keep the jewelry to a bare minimum.

Guys

- If you don't have or want to wear a sports jacket, that's fine. Wear a rugby shirt, button down, or basic sweater. But don't wear the clothes that have the designer's name written on the front or all over the outfit. Stick to light colors, and only a few. Too many colors won't cut it.
- Stop the sag. Khakis and corduroys are fine, but don't let them sag. Employers are not impressed by your boxers.
- Dress boots are okay if you are wearing khakis or cords, but not if you have on dress slacks.
- Wear a belt: it makes you look polished.
- If you have to wear jewelry, keep it to a minimum. If you have earrings, take them out, or at least wear no more than one.
- Keep the cologne to a minimum, if at all.
- No hats.

What about the hair? As with everything else, try to keep your hairstyle conservative.

- For ladies, nothing in your face or very dramatic. Keep the style simple and natural looking.
- For guys, make sure the style is clean. Avoid styles such as "puffs," cornrows, and designs in your fade. If you have longer hair, pull it back. If an Afro is your style, make sure that it's maintained properly. Don't go with it dry and tore-off looking. If dreds are your thing, tie them back.

Whatever you choose to do with your hair, just make sure that it looks polished and professional. Your whole appearance counts, not just the clothes you wear.

BONUS! Here's something to think about: Our sense of smell is a very powerful memory trigger. Think about yours. Do you remember someone specific whenever you smell a certain perfume or cologne or other smell? This is very common. Now, what if you walked into an interview wearing a scent that reminded your interviewer of someone they had a negative experience with? Now, this person probably would not look at you and judge you because of it, but it could cause for a big distraction during your interview, which you don't need. So, the best bet is to avoid fragrances altogether when you go to interview.

Remember: This is not a fashion show you are going to—it's a job interview. Employers don't care about fashion as much as your friends do. The interview needs to be focused on you and your skills, not how you look and smell. You don't want to wear things that will cause a distraction.

Role-Playing: Choose the Professional Style

Below are pictures of some people who are going for job interviews. It's your job to decide whether each is appropriately dressed for an interview. Look at each person, circle the problem areas, and in the space provided, write what would be more appropriate for an interview.

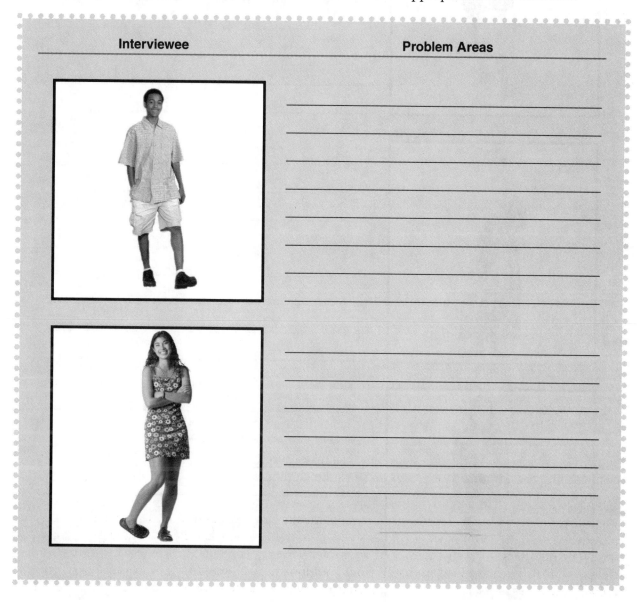

Interviewee **Problem Areas**

(continues)

(continued)

Interviewee	Problem Areas
	_____ _____ _____ _____ _____ _____ _____ _____
	_____ _____ _____ _____ _____ _____ _____ _____
	_____ _____ _____ _____ _____ _____ _____

holla' zone: *a place for you to let out your thoughts*

appearance is a big deal when it comes to the interview—and even working on the job. if you have trouble following the dress code, chances are you won't have that job for very long. take this time to write down your personal "requirements" for dressing on a job.

_____

_____

_____

Watch the Time

The first impression on an interview starts when you walk in the door, and the interviewer's watch sets the tone for the first impression. If you come in late or just barely on time, your interview will often be affected. Timeliness is an important factor in interviewing, as it says a lot about the type of employee you will be. Complete the following worksheet and then read on for more helpful hints on timeliness.

The following scenarios are situations that we come up against every day and are especially common when it comes to interviewing. Read through the scenarios and their corresponding choice of actions, and then decide which action you would take in the situation. Remember: Your goal is to make the best impression possible in your interview; you don't want to lose this job.

Scenario 1

You just got off the phone from scheduling a job interview. It's at 1:00 p.m. tomorrow, but you're not quite sure how you'll get there. Your mom is working so she can't take you and you would prefer not to have to take the bus, so you call your friend. Great! She agreed to take you, but she wants to know what time to be at your place to pick you up. This friend is really good about being places on time, so you know that she will be there at whatever time you decide. The interview is only 10 minutes from your place, so when should she be there?

❏ 12:15   ❏ 12:30

❏ 12:50   ❏ 12:45

Scenario 2

You're scheduled to leave for your interview at 2:00 p.m. The interview is at 2:45 p.m., and the place is 20 minutes away. It's 1:55 p.m., and you just found out that the car won't run. You've called all your friends, and no one can pick you up. You could take public transportation, but it will take at least one hour to get there on the bus. What are you going to do?

❑ Get on the bus. If you catch it now, you may make it there in less that an hour.

❑ Call the employer, explain the situation, and reschedule the interview for another day.

❑ Call the employer, explain the situation, tell him or her that you will be taking the bus so you may be a few minutes late, and ask if that would be a problem. Thank him or her for being understanding and working with your situation.

❑ Just forget about the interview; it must not have been meant to be.

Scenario 3

You've had your interview scheduled since last week. You have been preparing yourself, and you feel ready for the interview. The day before the interview, your family gets a phone call. Your uncle unexpectedly died in his sleep the night before, and you have to leave town for the funeral. Amid all the hurry to leave, you completely forgot about your interview, so you didn't call to cancel. It wasn't until two days later that you remembered the interview. The interview date has passed, and you didn't let anyone know what was going on. Is it too late? What should you do?

❑ Call the employer, apologize for missing the interview and not even calling to inform him or her, and explain what happened. Then ask if there is any way to reschedule the interview.

❑ Forget about the entire interview. There is no point in calling as the employer already thinks negatively about you for not showing up.

❑ Call the employer and tell him or her you were just calling to apologize for missing the interview and that you hope it didn't cause too many problems in their schedule.

❑ Call the employer and try to set up a new interview. Just say that you are interested in the position and would like to set an interview. Don't tell them you missed the interview. They probably won't even realize you missed your first interview.

Scenario 4

You set up an interview last week, but the more you think about the job you are applying for, the more you realize that it's not really what you want. The interview is tomorrow, but you don't really want to go. What do you do?

❑ Call the employer, and make up some excuse for not being able to make it to the interview. If the person asks if you would like to reschedule, tell him that you have to check your schedule, which you don't have with you at the moment, so you'll have to get back to him, and then never call back.

❑ Just don't show up for the interview.

❑ Go to the interview, but come across as highly uninterested so they don't ask to hire you.

❑ Call the employer and explain that you are no longer interested in the position, cancel the interview, and then thank her for setting time to meet with you and understanding your change of mind.

When you are going to an interview, it is important that you know exactly where you are going, how long it will take to get there, and know alternative ways to get to the interview. In addition, you want to be in communication with the interviewer if a problem arises.

Tips to Keep in Mind When Dealing with Time for an Interview

- Arrive at least 10 minutes before the interview.

- At all costs, avoid being late.

- Time how long it takes to get to the business a day or two before the interview. (Take your test-drive around the same time you will be interviewing. Traffic varies throughout the day.)

- If you are not driving yourself, make sure that whoever is driving you is dependable and on time. If you know someone who is always late, don't ask that person for a ride.

- If an emergency arises and you are going to be late, call as soon as you can to let the employer know. Try to keep your interview, but if you are really behind, and it will conflict with other business, reschedule for the following day.

- If you miss your interview and are unable to call before the interview, call as soon as you can. If you are still interested in the position, explain the situation and ask if you can reschedule. Many times if you are honest and show you are really interested, you will get another opportunity.

- If, after scheduling your interview, you decide that you do not want the job, call the employer, thank him/her for the opportunity to interview, and explain that you have decided that you are not interested in the position anymore, so you are canceling the appointment. Never just don't show up for an interview.

BONUS! Arriving early to an interview not only looks good to an employer, but also will allow you some extra time to prepare. Here are some other benefits:

- Gives you time to collect yourself and relax before the interview

- Provides time to investigate and find out more about the company, as you will often find literature and other information about the company in the waiting area

- Allows you to fix your hair, clothes, makeup, or anything else that may be out of place from the commute

- Lets you check out the work environment to see whether it's a place you would feel comfortable working in

holla' zone: **a place for you to let out your thoughts**

your timeliness for an interview says a lot about your work ethic and other areas of your life. are there other situations in your life in which timing is an important to your success? where and why?

_____

_____

_____

_____

_____

What to Do During the Interview

You thought you could play it cool once you got past the first impression. You figured that, provided you answered all the questions correctly, there was really nothing else to worry about during the actual interview. Sorry, it's not quite so easy. It's sort of like when you were little and your family went someplace special. There were certain things that you would always do around the house that Mom wouldn't allow you to do while at the special place. But trying to remain on your best behavior during an interview without being nervous is not always easy.

Be on Your Best Behavior in the Interview

Following is a list of behaviors that people have a tendency to do during an interview that could be done differently. Many of these are okay, but other behaviors are more effective.

Read over each item in the worksheet. In the line next to it, write in a more appropriate action or response.

Response	More Appropriate Response
1. Start and end the interview with a soft handshake.	_____
2. Look at the floor or the wall behind your interviewer throughout the interview.	_____

3. Keep a big smile pasted across your face throughout the interview. _____

4. Cross your arms and get comfortable in your seat. _____

5. Respond quickly and softly to all questions. _____

6. When you're nervous, tap your foot under the table. No one will notice. _____

7. Never say, "I don't know." If you're really unsure of an answer, just make something up. _____

8. Avoid talking about any weaknesses you may have. _____

9. You should be yourself at all times, so it's okay to use slang if that's how you talk. _____

10. As soon the interviewer asks if you have any questions, ask about your pay. _____

Here's the lowdown on what you should and shouldn't do during the interview.

● Have a firm handshake at the beginning and end of the interview.

● Avoid the light, delicate handshake and the powerful, over-the-top, controlling handshake. Give a firm, full-handed handshake.

● Start the interview off on a positive note by complimenting something about the office or the person you are interviewing, but be real.

- Thank the interviewer for the opportunity to meet with him or her.

- Make eye contact–don't stare down the interviewer, but do make eye contact throughout the interview.

- Be real throughout the interview. Smile, but don't fake it.

- Be aware of your posture–no slouching in your chair. Sit up straight, feet on the ground, hands either to your sides or folded on the table or desk in front of you.

- Pace your answers (don't talk too fast).

- After the employer asks you a question, pause for a few seconds to reflect on what was asked so that you can answer appropriately.

- Listen carefully. Pay attention to and thoroughly absorb what the other person is saying; they will often tell you exactly what they're looking for in an employee.

- Avoid distracting mannerisms such as foot tapping or running your hands through your hair.

- If you are nervous, take subtle deep breaths while the interviewer is talking. If you calmly breath in deep (but quietly) through your nose and out slowly through your mouth, your deep breathing exercises will hardly be noticed and you'll be able to relax quickly.

- Even though you may be nervous, try to respond to all questions in a calm, clear, and even tone. Make sure your voice is loud enough to be heard, but don't yell at the employer.

- If you don't know an answer, it is okay to respond, "I don't know," but follow the statement up with a response that shows what you might do or how you would work to find an answer to the question.

  Example: If the employer asks what you would do in a particular situation, you may say, "I have never been in that situation so I don't know exactly what I would do, but I know that I would do everything I could to make sure the customer is satisfied provided that I didn't overstep company policy."

- Always answer questions honestly and openly, but be prepared to defend any weaknesses with examples of how you're working to improve.

- Don't feel the need to answer questions with answers you think the employer wants to hear. Answer according to you feel is right and appropriate for you.

  Example: If employer asks you if you can work on Sundays and you can't for family reasons, don't say you can just to get the job.

- Interviewing is part of a game, and in this game there are certain rules. While you don't have to be somebody you're not, you do have to play your part to get the position. Slang, "uh-huh," "huh," "um," and saying things are "bogus," are just some of the "no-no's" to getting a job.

- Don't bring up the issue of pay until after you have been offered the position.

Close with a Thank-You

When you've finished asking and answering questions, the interview isn't over yet. What you do before and after you leave the office are some of the most important steps to getting the job. If you're worried about what to do at the end, keep these simple steps in mind:

1. Show interest—if you want the job.

   The end of the interview is your time to close with a positive, "I'm very interested in what you have learned" type close. When the interviewer has closed with "If you have no further questions, then we are done," that is your cue to say one of the following:

   - Actually, I'd like to know how I should proceed from here. Should I contact you, or will you be in contact?

   - How soon will I hear from you?

   - What is the process from here?

   - What would distinguish one potential candidate joining your company from another?

   - How do I prove my commitment to the organization?

2. Thank the interviewer.

   Regardless of how well or how poorly you feel things went, remain friendly and courteous to the interviewer, and thank him or her for taking time to meet you.

Don't Get Discouraged

You went to the interview with confidence, answered the questions to the best of your ability, and knew that you would be perfect for the job, but you didn't get hired. Or maybe you didn't even get past the phone conversation before the employer showed no interest in meeting with you. You think the employer didn't like you because of your age, past, or whatever. It's beginning to look like you will never get a job; maybe you are doing something wrong. Maybe, but probably not.

If you think that an employer didn't hire you because of your age, past, or whatever, well, maybe it's true, but not necessarily. Even if it were so, don't get discouraged. You would not have wanted to work in that environment anyway. You want to work where your supervisor understands you and is willing to work with you. No one should have to work at a job where their employer doesn't appreciate the employees' work. If you know that you could have done an excellent job in that position but you weren't hired, then *the employer* lost out, not you.

A better job is probably out there for you. Just keep looking and use the techniques you have learned in this workbook to help you find a job. You *will* find a job. If you know what you could have done better or you need to gain more skills before getting that kind of a job, then look at being turned down as an opportunity to learn how you can improve your skills—whether in interviewing or in specific skills for the job. Always look at what you've done as a learning experience, no matter what the result. If you can learn from it rather than just walk away mad, you will make a better employee in the long run. After you get a job, you will have disappointments at times and if you can't work through those, it will be hard for you to keep any job.

Remember: No matter how good or bad an impression you made, you're not always going to get the job. Sometimes you may think the interview was lousy and you won't be hired, but don't let that stop you from following up with a call and thank-you note if you really want the job.

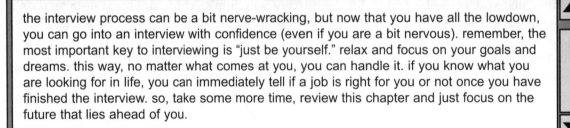

holla' zone: *a place for you to let out your thoughts*

throughout this entire chapter, you've learned different techniques to improve your chances of getting a job, but none of these steps guarantee that the job is yours. not getting a job, especially the job you want, can be difficult. it gets even more difficult when you get turned down again and again. for this holla' zone, write some ways that you can stay encouraged throughout the entire process.

_____

_____

_____

_____

_____

meta - Instant Message

the interview process can be a bit nerve-wracking, but now that you have all the lowdown, you can go into an interview with confidence (even if you are a bit nervous). remember, the most important key to interviewing is "just be yourself." relax and focus on your goals and dreams. this way, no matter what comes at you, you can handle it. if you know what you are looking for in life, you can immediately tell if a job is right for you or not once you have finished the interview. so, take some more time, review this chapter and just focus on the future that lies ahead of you.

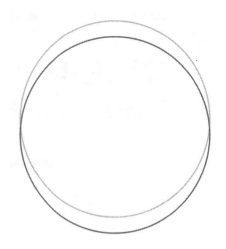

Answers to Activities

Chapter 1

Scrambled Words

1. goals
2. application
3. resume
4. fired
5. classified ads
6. interview
7. networking
8. internship
9. grants
10. armed services
11. loans
12. community college
13. trade school
14. diploma
15. entrepreneurial
16. FAFSA

Be Whatcha Wanna Be

1. f
2. q
3. a
4. m
5. n
6. d
7. o
8. e
9. k
10. g
11. h
12. i
13. j
14. p
15. b
16. l
17. c

Chapter 2
Everyone Has Options

```
R E D I V O R P E R A C D L I H C C O G Y H I A
L O N H C E P H E T O G R P H O T O G R A P H Y
E E A T A C I O M U S I K F S D A N C A E E O H
C D I W R N A T D R M M B A S G I S A P C L T F
T A L Y M U S I C G E A D S C B S T S H H E E K
E N T R E P R E N E U R S H I P T R A I N I N G
C C E C D A R T N E P E U I N O I T A C U D E P
H E C L S R M N R T T N S O A T E G S A I C M T
N H H A E A E D U K R A H N H R D N O R L T A R
O O N S R L D E C R O E I D C A C I C T D R S W
L T I S V E I N T H S H N E E N A B I D C I S S
O E C I I G C T I O L I E S M I T M A E A C A E
G L I E C A A E O T O E N I E N I U R S R I G S
Y M A S E L E L N E G M S G C G O L E I E A E S
E E N E L E C T R I C I A N H I N P A G Z Z T A
L N D D E N T A L A S S I S T A N T L N W Y H L
E A H O T E L M A N A G E M E N T V E V V R E C
C G F C H I L D C A Y G O L O T E M S O C A R E
N U R S I N G I F I L M P R O D U C T I O N A N
E M L E E R G E D S E T A I C O S S A I D I P I
C E M M E D I C A L A S S I S T A N T E M L I L
A A R T A N D D E S I G N C O S M E E T O U S N
N C O N S T R U C T N O I T C U R T S N O C T O
```

Chapter 4
True or False Personal Data

1. True

2. False (Write NA for Not Applicable.)

3. True

4. False (Take two applications. Complete the first one in pencil, but do the second one in pen and turn that one in.)

5. False (Never abbreviate anything.)

6. False (Read through the whole application to make sure you fill out only the parts that are required.)

7. False (Make sure the application is neat and clean.)

8. True

9. False (You are not required to.)

10. True

Personal Data

1. False (Use your full, legal name, not nicknames.)

2. True

3. True

4. False (Put "Open" or "Negotiable.")

5. False (Put an exact date or "Immediately" if you can start right away.)

Referral Source
1. d

Travel
2. a

References
3. b, c, d

4. a, c, d

Working Status
1. c

2. a

3. b

Shifts
1. c

2. b

3. d

4. a

Chapter 6
Role-Playing
Interviewee 1
This laid-back, sharp brotha' looks fly for a night out with the guys, but if he wants to impress an employer, it will take more than his "shy-guy" smile to get him a job. All's it takes is a tucked-in shirt and some khakis and he'll be good to go.

Interviewee 2
Okay, this is not a beach party she's going to. This outfit is a little too short and revealing for an interview. And her posture—it does nothing to convey confidence in herself to an employer. A

longer dress and a button-down sweater would be a better option for her; combine it with some flats and she would make a good candidate.

Interviewee 3
He walks in the door like this, and he'll be right back on the bus stop in no time! This guy does nothing to create the professional appeal. First, he needs to drop the attitude. No business wants to hire a "punk"; they're looking for someone who's cheerful, respectful, and confident. And the clothes! Man, he needs to lose that baggy sweater, ditch the saggy jeans, and think about getting some dress boots. A nice pair of cords and a loose sweater with some dress boots would help clean up the image a bit. As for the hair, that could be fixed a bit as well.

Interviewee 4
She's almost got it together for an interview. She has on a nice dress, her hair is neat, and she's really smiling. Really the only thing out of place is the shoes. Sandals are a bit too casual for an interview. One more thing, the jean vest may not be the best option for the interview as well.

Interviewee 5
Girlfriend, you're really cute, but to get a job you'll have to grow up some. Employers don't fall for that "innocent little girl" look. The braids are cute, but too young-looking for an interview. Try pulling it back in a pony tail or just wearing it straight. And the jeans, you know that's a "no-no." The sweater passes, but the jacket shouldn't be kept on for the interview. If you want to wear it, take it off after you get in the front door.

Watch the Time

Scenario 1
12:30

Scenario 2
Either the second or third options

Scenario 3
The first option: Call, apologize, explain, and try to reschedule.

Scenario 4
The last option: Explain that you're not interested and thank the person.

Be on Your Best Behavior in the Interview

1. Give a firm, full handshake.

2. Make eye contact throughout the interview.

3. Smile when appropriate but don't fake it.

4. Sit up straight with your arms to your side or on the desk in front of you.

5. Pause before responding. Speak loudly enough to be heard.

6. Avoid tapping your foot. If you're nervous, take subtle, deep breaths.

7. It's okay to say "I don't know," but follow with a response that shows your willingness to learn.

8. Turn weaknesses into strengths.

9. Be yourself, but avoid slang.

10. The issue of your pay is answered after you've been offered the position.

Index

experience, 161
failures, 189
fears, overcoming, 10
goal setting, 100
goals, personal, 35
interviewing, 185
nervousness, 194
networking, 129
purpose, finding, 17
sacrifices, 85-86
scholarships, 68
school choices, 74
school planning, 71
self-marketing, 146
skills, gaining, 119
staying in school, 85-86
success, defining, 35
teamwork, 91-92
thank-you notes, 176-177
timeliness, 206
training, 60
volunteering, 21-22
hotjobs.com, 122

I

interests, 6-7
career guide, 24-30
international schools, 41
Internet, 120, 122-123
internship, 5
interviews, 5, 141-145, 179-210
behavior, 206-208
characteristics to demonstrate, 189
closing, 209
cologne, 200
company information, 184
discouragement, 209-210
discrimination, 193
dress codes, 198-203
eagerness, 183-184
eye contact, 208
experiences, 182-183, 187
goals, 182
handshakes, 207
passion, 183-184
pay discussion, 208
perseverance, 186-187
phone, 142-145
positives vs. negatives, 186
posture, 208

preparing for, 179-194
questioning the company, 195-197
business-related, 195
general, 195
personal, 195
scripts, 197
questions, 180-184, 189-197
education, 190-191
future-related, 192
general, 190
inappropriate, 193-194
work-related, 191-192
respect, 187-188
self-promotion, 179-181
strengths, 186
style, 201-202
timeliness, 203-205
two-minute story, 181, 184-185
weaknesses, 186-189

J-L

job search, see career search

leadership skills, 101-105
assertiveness, 102
community issues, 104-105
desire to excel, 102
knowledge, 102
liberal arts colleges, 41, 54
life planning, 3-35
careers, 23-35
defining success, 15-17
dreams, 8-9
fears, overcoming, 10-11
game of life, 4-11
personal success, 12
success, 11-18
volunteering, 19-22
loans, 5, 64

M-N

mission, defined, 18
career search as, 18
money as motivator, 11-12
monster.com, 122
motivation, 11-12, 80
music therapist, 23

networking, 5, 114, 124-129
building, 126-127
defined, 124
good judgment and, 126
honesty and, 126
resources, 125
trustworthiness, 126
Two-Foot Rule, 125
understanding, 128-129

O-P

Occupational Outlook Handbook, 31
odd jobs, 109
on-line colleges, 41

patience, 79-86
perseverance, 186-187
personal success, 12
personal trainer, 24
phone etiquette, 141-146
answering machine messages, 145
business calls, 145
interviews, 142-145
posture, 208
Practice Makes Perfect activities, 1
answering interview questions, 190
asking questions, 196
cover letter, 167
goal setting, 95
networking, 128
references, 160
resumes, 158-159
thank-you notes, 170
two-minute story, 184
private investigator, 24
publicity consultant, 23
purpose, finding, 17-18

Q

questions, interview, 180-184, 189-197
education, 190-191
future-related, 192
general, 190
inappropriate, 193-194
work-related, 191-192